Mere Believers

Mere Believers

How Eight Faithful Lives
Changed the Course of History

Marc Baer

CASCADE *Books* · Eugene, Oregon

MERE BELIEVERS
How Eight Faithful Lives Changed the Course of History

Cascade Books
An Imprint of Wipf and Stock Publishers
199 W. 8th Ave., Suite 3
Eugene, OR 97401

www.wipfandstock.com

ISBN 13: 978-1-62564-205-9

Cataloguing-in-Publication Data

Baer, Marc.

Mere believers : how eight faithful lives changed the course of history / Marc Baer.

xviii + 172 p. ; 23 cm. Includes bibliographical references.

ISBN 13: 978-1-62564-205-9

1. Biography—Religious aspects—Christianity—History—18th century to 20th century. 2. Christian converts—England—Biography—History and criticism. I. Title.

BR758 .B2 2013

Manufactured in the U.S.A.

To some cherished believers, my children
—Brett, Carter, Jaime—
and their families.

Contents

Illustrations

Acknowledgments

As THE INTRODUCTION WILL make clear, although everything else I've written during my career as an academic had in mind an audience of scholars, *Mere Believers* is intended for a general readership. Scholars who happen on it may go to my personal website for details on the research.

Given the manner in which I brought the book to completion I have a number of organizations and individuals to thank. Chapters 3, 4, and 5 began life as talks at the 2003 InterVarsity Christian Fellowship Great Lakes East staff conference. Thanks to two grants from the Hope College Cross-Roads Project (funded by the Lilly Endowment), I was able to work with and learn from Hope College students Brianne Carpenter on the Dorothy Sayers chapter and Andreas Van Denend on G. K. Chesterton. The Huntingdon and Equiano chapters were written during sabbaticals, for which I'm grateful to Hope. Ian Bussan performed admirably as a footnote detective, while Sarah Baar helped with formatting the final manuscript. My agent John Topliff encouraged me during the final years of the project, and Rodney Clapp at Wipf and Stock helped me think through a number of matters.

Ann Loades read the Sayers chapter and provided helpful comments. Bob Shuster and Keith Call at the Wheaton College Archives helped the research on the Chambers go smoothly. A great many individuals whose names I can't recall read or heard versions of most of the chapters, and their comments have helped me enormously: this includes audiences at Cedar Campus InterVarsity faculty conferences in 2006 and 2010; the 2009 Baylor Symposium on Faith and Culture; the 2011 and 2013 versions of my Hope College senior seminar, Exploring Faith and Calling; and the adult Sunday school class at Pillar Church in Holland, Michigan. And, as with all my books, my wife Patricia took time away from her professional responsibilities to read and comment on each chapter. The book—and my life—are better because of her.

Introduction

The Bible says that when you become a Christian your mind is renewed,
and so that with that renewing of your mind
comes a new view of the world in which you live.
László Tőkés

WILLIAM WILBERFORCE DEFINED *CHRISTIAN* as "a pilgrim travelling on business through a strange country."[1] The pages that follow examine eight such pilgrims from Britain's past, the society I've been studying for the last forty-five years, asking this question: Did their Christianity change their country? Led to travel on business, as Wilberforce phrased it, did reorienting their hearts and minds result in any measureable consequences for their culture? Was the world better or worse because of them? Philosophers, atheists, and my fifteen-year-old nephew are raising these very questions today, and so I've invited some believers from the past to brief us—or rather, for us to interview them.

My interest in the questions arose out of my own story. Like my subjects I became a believer as an adult. My parents were Unitarians, my father growing up in and then forsaking a tiny denomination of German and Swiss Protestants and my mother as an unbelieving Jewish Ukrainian immigrant who dabbled in Theosophy. They met in graduate school, which meant that acquisition of knowledge was highly valued in my clan. Having been raised in California, my family moved to Iowa when I was in high school. With such a background of course I was going to ask questions! Having rejected the worldview of my parents, determining somewhere between California and Iowa that at best one religion might be true but reasonably not all them could possibly be true, by the time I entered college I was a committed non-believer who nevertheless had a nagging doubt about his doubts. The

1. Spring, "Clapham Sect," 40.

best I could do was to sense what was false. Years later I would hear G. K. Chesterton say that "Truth can understand error; but error cannot understand Truth."[2]

In this season of searching I let my doubts carry me into a philosophy minor to complement my history major. Studying the world's religions and their texts—the *Koran* and the *Bhagavad-Gita*, the *Tao Te Ching* and *The Teachings of the Compassionate Buddha*, as well as Christianity and the Bible—confirmed my jejune feeling that in fact *none* of them was true. It was not until halfway through graduate school that I had the desire—or perhaps it was courage—to ponder the more profound question: did any of the texts reveal what I knew to be true about myself? That no rhyme accompanied my reason, the ideas about humanity next to the knowledge about the one human I knew all too well, led me to read the Bible for the first time asking *that* question. Following over a year of reflection I became a believer—by which I understood what the biblical writer Paul had: "if you confess with your mouth, 'Jesus is Lord,' and believe in your heart that God raised him from the dead, you will be saved" (Romans 10:9, ESV).

Traveling without as I was changing within, I took on beliefs at odds with who I had been, because to be a follower of Jesus is to believe what he believed. That human beings were created in the image of God caused me to change how I thought about people—especially the most vulnerable; realizing that I hadn't earned anything caused me to change what I thought about my possessions; and realizing that loving God with my mind sometimes meant having to confront the spirit of the age but also sometimes meant having to go to war with my own precious worldview. Since as an academic I think for a living, pretty much every day I need to remind myself that Jesus didn't say, "Decide for me." Rather, he said "Come to me." And the big one, from before I became a believer to now forty-two years later: the church drives me nuts. But as a historian it's clear that God uses the church in his project to redeem humankind. While God needs me like you need a toothache, it's his plan, and here's the test: take the church out of history and ask, as honestly as you can what the world would be like. Are there good things like art, hospitals, literature, science, universities and education for the poor? So I had better love the church even if I don't always like it, and loving includes knowing about who created those good things—and why.

From the moment my spiritual journey began in my twenty-fifth year I have been intrigued with other lives as parables, as Oswald Chambers,

---

2. Chesterton, *Autobiography*, 248.

another subject of this book, once put it. Given my curiosity about how individuals shape their cultures, governments, and societies, the book's central question began to take shape. I set out to use the place I knew best—modern Britain—to see if a critical historian's rather than a philosopher's or theologian's understanding might help readers understand whether Christian belief has had an impact more good than evil, so that they might understand whether our present world is better with all these pilgrims than it would have been without them. Throughout the research for this book I have used the same scholarly approach as for all my other academic work—reading original sources and the best and most recent scholarship on the subjects.

Why these eight figures? First, because they are a diverse lot, letting them become in the words of C. S. Lewis, "merely Christian." They are male and female, black and white, rich and poor. They are English, Welsh, Scots, and an African immigrant. They lived in the eighteenth, the nineteenth, and the twentieth centuries. And they represent a variety of Christian traditions: Catholic; virtually every point on the Anglican theological spectrum; and several Nonconformist denominations. Only one was ordained, for I wanted to consider individuals whose vocations were worldly.

Second, in previous scholarly research I had encountered them and in almost every instance felt dissatisfied by what I read. Frankly, the Christian work on them lacks critical analysis of the evidence. It was not simply that non-academics don't have the training and practice to carry out empirical research. Beyond that, the characters came across as one-dimensional, enervated and too good to be true because some of the layers of their lives were left unexplored or at least under-reported. In the chapters that follow readers will encounter believers who were suicidal, addicted to drugs, abusers of alcohol, promiscuous, plagued with doubt, or overly zealous and authoritarian. In trying to be transparent about faults as well as faith I hope they come across as real because they remind us of ourselves—less than perfect souls longing for our own and humanity's flourishing. But because they went beyond the cultural roles and personal problems dealt to them they reveal how our choices might define us rather than our experiences—that ideas certainly do have consequences.

Where it existed I remained underwhelmed by much of the scholarly work on my subjects. Too often they were made to serve another agenda. In response, my approach was to make them neither better nor worse than the story told by the surviving documents. Throughout I have tried the best

I could to let them speak in their own words, so that they would be able to recognize themselves in my words.

Third, individually and collectively the eight characters allow reflection on hearts and minds at work in human history, to ponder how belief connects to behavior, and to test what is to me as an academic the most important teaching of Jesus. A teacher of Jewish law had heard Jesus give a particularly profound answer in a debate, and so had asked him, "Of all the commandments, which is the most important? 'The most important one,' answered Jesus, 'is this: 'Hear, O Israel, the Lord our God, the Lord is one. Love the Lord your God with all your heart and with all your soul and with all your mind and with all your strength.' The second is this: 'Love your neighbor as yourself. There is no commandment greater than these'" (Mark 12:31, NIV). In connecting hearts and minds, emotion and intellect, Jesus understood humans—as we may apprehend the one human each of us knows best—more profoundly than any theorist at work now or in the past. Moving beyond a self-referential attitude is the crux of our journey from narcissism to a more expansive self. Believers are people who recognize God is greater than Me, but also that We is greater than Me.

Finally, I wanted to spend time reflecting on these eight individuals because more and more I encounter people—students, colleagues, neighbors, writers—whose beliefs about human rights and human dignity, about social justice and freedom, seem to suppose that these are somehow the inevitable result of moral evolution. They appear unaware of their connections to historical individuals whose Christian convictions followed up belief with action and so revolutionized opinions in the past. In my work as a historian it's rather hard to discern any consistent evidence for moral evolution, regardless of the commonly held assumptions today that *of course* we are smarter, less superstitious, more caring and thoughtful than those who have gone before. Historians term such claims *presentism*, and in fact they are a hindrance to moral evolution rather than its proof. That which is not true should never be comforting. So it is that almost all people in the present are believers—even atheists—because the way they view the world *morally* was shaped by people in the past. Those people believed so strongly that God is love and that history has a purpose that they went out and changed their world. Their actions deflected history from paths that would have brought us to very different places than we see today.

Not in opposition but more like the layering of a palimpsest I set out to ask different questions of my four subjects drawn from the mid-eighteenth through the early nineteenth centuries—the countess of Huntingdon, Olaudah Equiano, Hannah More, and William Wilberforce—in contrast to my four late nineteenth to mid-twentieth century subjects—Oswald and Biddy Chambers, G. K. Chesterton, and Dorothy Sayers. For the first set, I wanted to explore what happens to *hearts* after conversion. The concern was drawn from a letter Paul wrote to the church in the city of Rome:

> Love must be sincere. Hate what is evil; cling to what is good. Be devoted to one another in brotherly love. Honor one another above yourselves. Never be lacking in zeal, but keep your spiritual fervor, serving the Lord (Rom 12:9–11, NIV).

Hence the question on the minds of every generation from Baby Boomers to Millennials: Can I give my heart to that?

For the second group I wanted to understand what happens to *minds* after conversion. In that same letter of Paul is this charge: "Do not conform any longer to the pattern of this world, but be transformed by the renewing of your mind" (Rom 12:2, NIV). Hence the question common on campus and around the office or the food truck, one I certainly asked before I was a believer: Does becoming a Christian mean I have to give up thinking for myself? I once knew an endless number of ways to claim that Christians were intellectually inferior to the best minds in history. I used some variant of the argument on every believer I encountered until I blundered by trying it out on someone who rather than taking offense challenged me to test my argument by seriously engaging the Bible. I was so shaken by what I read that a few days after passing my PhD comprehensive exams—when in some ways I grasped the knowledge of my field better than I would ever again—I asked God to become my teacher. Since then I've learned that many intellectuals come to faith the way they do everything else, thinking their way to a solution, and that this has been true for some of the best minds of every age. Chambers, Chesterton, and Sayers are three of them.

The chief problem with expressions of embitterment directed at religions or spiritual people is that strong opinions are often coupled with weak expertise; frequently their foundation is flimsy if not outright fiction. Take the case that religion causes violence, and that banishing religion would promote peace. Recently I read an editorial in the *Washington Post*, written by a pundit with whom I'm usually in agreement. I'm amening up to the point when he exploded into this rant:

> All over the world, people murder in the name of God. Europe
> was once drenched in the blood of unbelievers, dissident believers,
> nonbelievers—believers who worship on the wrong day or in the
> wrong posture or in the wrong words. More bodies can be piled on
> the head of a pin than angels can dance on it.[3]

If one hit the delete key for the entire twentieth century the commentator would still be wrong. We can forget about the slam-dunk cases of the
disasters that befell humankind from individuals like Stalin or Hitler or
Mao who lived lives *away* from God; just ponder Pol Pot, and do the math.

Or take this review of a book whose contention is the necessity of
atheism if the human race is to advance, in the reviewer's words, "to the
level we were meant to achieve."[4] Other than the illogic of the two con-
structs *atheism* and *meant to achieve* appearing in the same sentence, the
opinion is widely held that the world has been worse because of the beliefs
of believers and would be better off with unbelief. If we are ever to think
our way toward a reasonable answer to that question, we need to know the
historical record better than I'm afraid most of us do.

I'll leave it to other historians to tell the story of how we've been here
before—the eighteenth-century Enlightenment, nineteenth-century isms
such as positivism and materialism, and twentieth-century totalitarian-
ism—all of which attacked religion waving the banner of progress, thus
making the so-called "new atheism" look rather like a horse and buggy.
History since the age of Christ is littered with the wreckage of ideas that
proposed something *higher* than loving God with heart and mind, something *more human*, something *more reasonable*, something *more true*,
something *more profound*, something *more respectable*, something *more
powerful*, something *more . . . good*. They have all failed the only test that
matters: as a consequence of any of these, are human beings more robustly
human, neither becoming atomized individuals adrift in a tiny boat all by
themselves nor slaves to stuff or the tyranny of the state?

The unfailing error of every ideologue past and present I've encountered lies in thinking that humans were created for ideas, rather than ideas
being created for humans. Realizing these failures is the antidote to the
problem of presentism, but again, this must be the work of others. Yet I

---

3. Richard Cohen, "Mitt Romney's faith is his business," *Washington Post,* June 4,
2012.

4. Amazon review.

can't help but quote these lines from Tennyson's *In Memoriam* (1849)—because poets generally see so clearly.

> Our little systems have their day;
>   They have their day and cease to be:
>   They are but broken lights of thee,
> And thou, O Lord, art more than they.

And so in my own case I changed my mind. Having hung out in graduate school on the fringes of Students for a Democratic Society I came to doubt whether ideologies ever really help people. Christians and other believers share much with socialists because they read this Old Testament proverb: "Do not withhold good from those who deserve it, when it is in your power to act" (Prov 3:27, NIV). Like Marx or me, most of the socialists I knew of didn't much like people, rather like the man Chesterton discovered who didn't like dogs but cared deeply for "the cause of Dogs."[5]

My goal for this book is to make its cast of characters and their stories better known, so that readers may find them helpful to their own thinking about the issues I've raised. Because their lives still matter insofar as they have shaped our own, in a way they can become our mentors. We all stand in need of mentors as we seek to apply our hearts and minds to our work in the world in which we live. Let them tug at you to see if it would make sense to adopt aspects of how they lived their lives because of how you would answer these questions: What if William Wilberforce had never become a believer, or what if he had never encountered other believers with whom he could carry out his abolitionist endeavors? On a likeliness scale, what would have been the probability that the slave trade would have been abolished in 1807—or ever?

By the end of the book's conclusion my hope is that readers will ask such questions of themselves and our own times. Do I move forward on a cause dear to me as a believer embedded in a community of believers, or can I remain uncommitted, because I'm far too righteous to spend time with the hypocrites in the church? Would such *independence*, if that's the right word, in fact thwart the very cause I felt so strongly about?

A few words about why the chapters are laid out as they are. Each begins with enough background on the subjects to place them in their historic and life contexts, prior to a segment on their conversion, pointing to how their lives were transformed. For each subject there is an image,

---

5. Ker, *Chesterton*, 347.

because invariably I want to know what historical characters looked like the better to connect to them. The chapter then moves to consider calling, as they struggled with the stage on which they should act, the use of gifts and resources they recognized they had, for example the great wealth of Selina Hastings in the first chapter. I included this segment because for a dozen years I have taught a seminar for college seniors on discerning vocation; the questions I've asked of my eight subjects I learned from having walked alongside many of my students in their explorations. The chapters then consider the achievements that followed conversion, how the person engaged in what we would consider counter-cultural actions, for example Olaudah Equiano, who challenged his contemporaries to reconsider their notions about people of color. Each chapter then finishes with a brief text written by the subjects to capture the flavor of their heart and mind, and then a handful of questions to engage the reader with the character.

On a ledge just beyond my desk, where I cannot avoid it each morning when I sit down, I've posted this line from Martin Luther King's *Letter from Birmingham City Jail*: "In those days the church was not merely a thermometer that recorded the ideas and principles of popular opinion; it was a thermostat that transformed the mores of society."[6] So the question before us, asked of one pilgrim in this book but appropriate for all of them: how was the trajectory of history different because some person in the past became a believer and what does that realization mean for me in my own time? If I'm truly passionate about peace, caring for creation, protecting children, encouraging racial reconciliation and social justice, might the very possibility of such longings rest on whether or not I love God with all my heart and my entire mind?

6. King, *Testament of Hope*, 300.

CHAPTER 1

Selina Hastings, Countess of Huntingdon

Story: The church—what is it?

> I am a poor individual called in faithfulness
> to take care of some hundred thousand souls.
> Selina Hastings, aged 83

IN 1768 SEVEN OXFORD students were tried before a university court for "holding Methodistical tenets, and taking upon them to pray, read and expound the Scriptures, and singing hymns in private houses," or, as one London newspaper stated a week later, "having too much religion."[1] Six of the seven were expelled from Oxford. In the universities, in the Church of England, in politics, and in society "enthusiasm" in the scornful expression of the day was the ruin of many a career or reputation. Into this maelstrom strode one enthusiast, a most unusual woman in that time or any, for few of her gender founded and managed a denomination, established a seminary, and personally lobbied George Washington—and in some ways these were the least of her accomplishments.

You do not need to like those sitting in the pew next to you, which makes the church distinctive. We may never have picked these people as our friends. Rather, they were chosen for us, as we were selected for them— and we are called to love them although we may not like them. Given how fearsome she could be, I would have been intimidated sitting next to Selina

---

1. Seymour, *Huntingdon*, i., 424.

Hastings in church or anywhere else for that matter. Nevertheless, as Cardinal Newman once remarked, believers of all times and persuasions have a great deal to learn from her.[2] What he had in mind was how the life of the Countess of Huntingdon connected to the passage wherein Jesus says to those who were true to what he taught, the church in the making, "For I was hungry and you gave me something to eat, I was thirsty and you gave me something to drink, I was a stranger and you invited me in, I needed clothes and you clothed me, I was sick and you looked after me, I was in prison and you came to visit me" (Matt 25:35–36). Noticing those in his audience were having a hard time applying this to themselves, Jesus clarified what he meant: "whatever you did for those the world overlooks, you did to me" (Matt 25:45).

So let's investigate her life by asking some questions: What actions should we take when the church is malfunctioning? When the institutional church will not tolerate us, or for that matter Jesus, what might we be called to do? How do we practice perseverance and courage in the face of trials and intimidation? Is multi-tasking rather than a narrower vocational focus harmful to our well-being?

Selina Shirley was born in 1707 into the privileged world of the English aristocracy, to a family able to trace its roots back more than seven centuries. One grandfather was ennobled, the other the Speaker of the Irish House of Commons. She was the middle of three daughters and co-heiresses of Washington Shirley, Earl Ferrers. Disinherited by his father—spawning decades of bitter litigation—the earl separated from his wife when Selina was six. Selina and one sister stayed with their father, living in relative privation in rural Ireland where as a soldier he was stationed. Her mother and another sister moved to France, and she never saw either of them again. After her father died, her mother sued and then disowned her. Frustrations from the promise of wealth coupled with unhappiness from family dynamics may explain her quick, even violent temper. She was a poor little rich girl if ever there was one.

Raised to be a fixture of high society, Selina's personality was on the earnest side in an age of frivolity and licentiousness. This was after all the Gin Age, when binge drinking was a national pastime. Said one churchman in 1734: "For about twenty years past, the English nation has been . . . so prodigiously debauched that I am almost a foreigner in my own country."[3]

2. Newman, "Selina, Countess of Huntingdon," 387–88.

3. Walsh, Haydon, and Taylor, *Church of England*, 21.

Deeply religious from an early age, Selina Shirley naturally became a do-gooder. As was the case with most women of the time, even wealthy ones, she had been poorly educated. Her thousands of letters reveal an individual well-read and thoughtful but far from having mastered the rules of the English language, while her illegible handwriting rivaled that of your doctor.

Just before turning twenty-one she married Theophilus Hastings, the wealthy ninth Earl of Huntingdon. The marriage produced a degree of happiness that had eluded Selina during her painful childhood. She bore her husband seven children in ten years, which may explain why she remained in poor health for the rest of her life.

The couple was well connected politically and socially—both were descended from English kings—part of a circle around the Prince of Wales, heir to the throne. They appeared frequently at the court of the prince's father, King George II. That her personality displayed fearlessness long before her conversion was evident in an episode in 1739 when with eleven other aristocratic women she stormed the House of Lords to protest the government's foreign policy.

Selina Hastings was religious, but not yet a believer, still relying on good works and using contemporary standards of living a moral life—in keeping with the values then exhibited by the Anglican Church, with its emphasis on decorum, moral duty, and human merit. The church had become as worldly as the world it had been intended to turn upside down, making it the problem rather than the solution.

Less than 50 percent of Anglican parishes had resident clergy, which denied much of the population access to meaningful worship. To make matters worse its theology was dysfunctional. Many of its best minds had turned their back on the church's spiritual heritage by privileging human reason against revelation, and as we've seen denigrating the joy expressed at the realization of personal assurance of salvation. Much of the preaching in the Church of England and other Protestant sects left many Britons, as it did John Newton, "weary of cold contemplative truths which cannot warm nor amend the heart."[4]

Then in the 1730s something unexpected happened. A revival began within the Church of England, famously recalled in John Wesley's experience: "I felt my heart strangely warmed."[5] Others before and after, not only in England but in Wales, Scotland, and Ireland had remarkably similar

4. Newton, *Works*, i, 85.
5. Wesley, *Journal*, 51.

conversion experiences, for example George Whitefield and Hwyel (Howell) Harris. Experience of the new birth generated fluidity and ferment, which was to be expected: rules and traditions went out the window; moral reformation was to follow upon spiritual regeneration.

The Wesley brothers, Whitefield, Harris, and others inside and outside the Church of England used new tools—large gatherings, spontaneous prayer, public confession of sin and expression of contrition, upbeat hymns, lay preaching, accountability groups open to anyone and, where relevant, itinerancy. The world was to be their parish rather than the other way round. "Methodist" came to be the label for a habit long before it was a denomination, characterized by a longing for a deeper spiritual life. Methodism began as a reform movement within Church of England and a coalition of the willing—which included Arminian followers of Wesley (emphasis on free will), Calvinist followers of Whitefield (emphasis on predestination), and Moravians (emphasis on personal piety).

Whenever extraordinary events occur, those in authority particularly feel threatened. The Methodist phenomenon was no different. One Anglican vicar termed it "this monstrous madness and religious frenzy," a "contagion" that he commented in relief was nevertheless confined to the dregs of society.[6] A bishop condemned Methodism for "its Tendency to undermine Morality and Good Works."[7] The title of a 1739 book says it all: *The nature, folly, sin, and danger of being righteous over-much; with a particular view to the doctrines and practices of certain modern enthusiasts.*

Now in her early thirties, the Countess of Huntingdon was aware of the upheaval but remained a mere observer. By then she had gained a husband but lost a baby, remained in poor health, and had been disowned by her mother. She exhibited good management skills, helping her husband administer his estates. This included prodding a number of tenants to pay rent in arrears, which provoked some resentment against her—the first of many experiences of hostility. She still relied on personal merit, failing to realize that at conversion, in the words of John Cennick, one of the converts of the 1730s, "all those fears, jealousies, and uneasinesses which generally, if not always, precedes it in the upright and sincere, are brought to an end."[8]

---

6. Tyerman, *Life and Times of John Wesley*, 328.

7. Wesley, *Works*, v., 395.

8. Hindmarsh, *Evangelical Conversion Narrative*, 89.

Conversion

The historic church teaches us that once an individual has a first-hand experience of Jesus, the old life loses its appeal. Those around us notice that we're different people, because recognition of truth reforms the way we think about ourselves and the world. Sometimes in history these individual reformations touch off larger Reformations; during the 1730s that was happening throughout the English-speaking world.

At the end of that decade Selina Hastings, aged thirty-two, experienced a life-threatening illness but as well a spiritual restlessness. Something seemed not quite right about her standing with God; she no longer felt assured by her own self-righteousness. She wrote to an acquaintance that she "wou'd undergoe every Thing to come to the true Knowledge of my only Saviour."[9]

In the midst of her illness she was cared for by her sister-in-law, Lady Margaret Hastings, who having heard Whitefield's preaching had experienced the new birth. Lady Margaret subsequently wrote Selina regarding her conversion: "Since I have known the Lord Jesus Christ for salvation, I have been as happy as an angel."[10] Placed alongside Selina's pride in her philanthropy, such joy was altogether new. Shortly thereafter the countess had some sort of experience—she never provided details—but her letters reveal the reality of justification by faith, that she had appropriated grace and now knew for certain that God had forgiven her. She had come to understand her good works flowed from—not to—faith, and she had obtained freedom from past thinking that salvation was something to be earned. Her husband the earl had some sort of spiritual rebirth as well.

Those around her noted a significant change, her maid commenting that she ceased losing her temper. When the Welsh itinerant preacher Howell Harris met her five years later he recalled that "one more delivered from her own will & wisdom I have Hardly seen."[11] And Philip Doddridge, a Congregational minister commented: "I think I never saw so much of the image of God in a woman on earth."[12] But many others thought she had gone off the deep end. She was advised by clergymen to be more moderate, not to pray too much, and to avoid taking on spiritual responsibilities.

9. Schlenther, *Huntingdon*, 16.

10. Seymour, *Huntingdon*, i., 14.

11. Nuttall, "Howel Harris," 531.

12. Doddridge, *Diary and Correspondence*, v., 171.

When an Anglican bishop, a friend of the family, spoke with her along these lines her response was to remind him what Christ expected of bishops, using both biblical texts and the Articles of the Church of England—an early sign of her confidence in her theological understanding.

Shortly after her conversion the countess began attending John Wesley's meetings in London. She also listened to and learned from the Moravians, one of whom found her "more eager to hear the gospel than anyone I ever saw before." He added: "She has a great liking for the [Moravian] Brethren; she does not lack good sense, but has a very violent temper,"[13] so that apparently that personality trait had not completed disappeared. George Whitefield, Charles Wesley, Howell Harris, and a female Quaker preacher were other sources of spiritual insight and counsel, but John Wesley especially was her lodestar. She wrote to him: "Nothing less do I look for from you than making our sinner, apostate Church the footstool of Christ. For this end . . . came . . . you and your brother into the world."[14] Whitefield diverged from Wesley and the countess on the role of predestination, and she once debated with Whitefield for several hours: "I told him I was so much happier than he was and that not from any thing in my self but on my Constant dependence upon Christ."[15] In locking horns with the most dramatic preacher of the time she once again displayed great confidence. But after nearly a decade of being drawn to the Wesleys the countess turned to Whitefield's theological understanding of the relationship between faith and works, signaled by appointing him as her chaplain.

Whitefield and those in his camp contended, based on their reading of the Bible, that only those chosen by God would be saved, while Wesley and other Arminians argued anyone could be saved. The biblical texts seem to support both positions: Jesus stated that "No one can come to me unless the Father who sent me draws him" (John 6:44); he also said "In my Father's house there's plenty of room" (John 14:2).

As the countess thought through this conundrum her approach was less theological than personal. The issue for her was whether love of God controls our intellect, because our intellect will certainly control our actions. Is our worldview an end or a means? How tightly must we hold onto it? Selina Hastings, the Wesleys and Whitefield, having experienced liberation, were all active evangelists, acting as if salvation was on offer to

13. Tyson and Schlenther, eds., *Early Methodism*, 48.

14. Ibid., 53.

15. Welch, *Spiritual Pilgrim*, 52.

everyone as it had been to them. Their role was to speak about their spiritual experience, rather than choosing to whom to speak. Thus it was that the countess told Charles Wesley that her modus operandi was to share the gospel with anyone she met regardless of social standing.

Conversion did not make the life of Selina Hastings perfect. She was to experience decades of despair. Her psychopathic cousin Lawrence Shirley, fourth Earl Ferrers, was executed in 1760 for the murder of his estranged wife's steward; convicted by a jury of his peers, the House of Lords, he was hanged at Tyburn, like a common criminal. After nineteen years of marriage in 1746 the countess's husband died suddenly, leaving her the responsibility for looking after his large estate and their surviving children. She later saw all but one of those children die; only her daughter Elizabeth survived the countess. Legal problems with her family of origin continued, as did her health problems, and she remained the butt of jokes.

But in spite of all these opportunities to grow weary and retreat, the changes that had characterized her life—from conspicuous consumption characteristic of her class to a new vision of how to invest her resources— produced perseverance and resiliency. One insight into this change is provided by the 1773 portrait she had commissioned for one of her American projects. In *The Right Honourable Selina, Countess Dowager of Huntingdon* the countess, now sixty-six, holds a crown of thorns while stepping on her coronet, the symbol of her rank. Her left hand holds up a fold of her simple dark gown, looking towards the viewer, with a plain white cloth over her head. Previous to her conversion a contemporary seeing her at court remarked on her dress, "I never saw so much finery."[16] Now plain dress symbolized, as she had written Charles Wesley, that serving God made one a servant not a master over others, while writing to his brother John that "I think no distinction of rank ought to be regard'd lest too

Selina Hastings, Countess of Huntingdon
After John Russell
© National Portrait Gallery, London

16. Granville, *Mrs. Delaney*, i., 167.

great a difference should be pay'd . . . more than the Christian of which we make our boast."[17] In the background of the portrait is a tree, the Tree of life. She stands before a sepulcher, likely a representation of the tomb of Jesus. Above is a plant, the common plantain, used as an herbal remedy—medicine being of great interest to her given her history of poor health. In William Shenstone's 1737 *The School-mistress* is this line: "And plantain rubb'd that heals the reaper's wound."[18] With its root structure entering the sepulcher, the message of the portrait may be, "Christ heals all wounds." Despite personal problems and criticisms of her work she had put off one crown—and one life—for another.

Calling

Imagine yourself a thirty-nine year-old widow with four young children and responsibility for managing your deceased husband's extensive properties spread around the country. What would you do in a situation where discouragement, depression, or turning inward spiritually would have been natural responses? Against expectations, the Countess of Huntingdon instead forged a new identity for herself by deepening the sense of calling that developed after her conversion a decade before her husband died. Knowing she was saved neither by anything she was nor by what she had done but instead by unmerited grace, her calling emerged out of a sense that her story should be shared with as many people as she could reach. She explored how that might be accomplished, doing so with unpredictable vigor. At times remarkably successful, on other occasions she experienced setbacks and condemnation. As calling needs to be secure, so the methods to achieve calling need to be flexible. And we should not be surprised when sometimes our very best efforts result in defeat.

The countess continued to face criticism for being public about her faith, most painfully from her own family. Her daughter Elizabeth thought her mother "righteous overmuch."[19] The countess's sister wrote her that she was

> sorry to find she Is turn'd Methodist as that sect Is so Generally exploded that It's become a Joke of all Compagnys . . . I'm Conserned

17. Tyson and Schlenther, *Early Methodism*, 59.
18. Shenstone, *Poetical Works*, 280.
19. Wesley, *Letters*, iv., 88.

to think my Dear Sister who Is so reasonable In every thing Else should Encourage such a Canttting set of people. . . . I hope God almighty who once endued you with a very good understanding will disperse the mist that now hangs before you and restore you to your former right way of judging.[20]

Such comments reflected growing distaste for Methodists among the well to do. Indeed, well into the next century William Wilberforce told his son that, "It is impossible for you to have any idea of the hatred in which the Methodists were then held."[21]

In spite of the criticism Selina Hastings chose to leverage her money and social position because of a new conviction that her resources did not belong to her. We should take note of how important it is to use Christian thinking as a counterweight to public opinion. Theologian William Law was one of her favorite authors. She certainly read chapter six of Law's 1728 book, *A Serious Call To a Devout and Holy Life*, entitled "The Wise Use of our Estates and Fortunes." In this the author asks readers to choose self-denial: "If we waste our money we are not only guilty of wasting a talent which God has given us but . . . we turn this useful talent into a powerful means of corrupting ourselves."[22] Charity must be a lifetime habit not an occasional hobby, which Law justifies by quoting the passage from Matthew with which this chapter began. Thus it was that a visitor to her home described it as "meanly furnished."[23] Part of the money that in the past might have been spent on herself went to prisoners who had been jailed for small debts: In 1749 along with her two sisters-in-law the countess visited debtors' prisons, personally helping thirty-four inmates out of her own pocket. She also funded schools, and engaged in personal evangelism, praying and singing with her servants and others. She reached out to laboring people in the vicinity of her estates, including coal miners.

She used her social position to protect ordained Methodists who were being harassed by the church establishment—in some dioceses they were blacklisted—and to expand their reach, in many cases complementing their work by calling lay preachers to join them. Early and then often the countess attempted to influence bishops to ordain men who she sensed had been

20. Tyson and Schlenther, *Early Methodism*, 34.
21. Furneaux, *Wilberforce*, 5.
22. Law, *Serious Call*, 52.
23. Seymour, *Huntingdon*, ii., 519.

called by the Holy Spirit to preach but who lacked the normal educational and social credentials for ordination.

Before the death of her husband the countess essentially invented a ministry to fellow nobles, using what might be understood as religious house parties. Having appointed Whitefield as her personal chaplain, she then invited the rich and powerful to her home to hear him or others such as John Wesley preach. She was summoning those she knew best and cared about to hear the gospel that had so transformed her own life. Whitefield recalled, "Last Sunday evening I preached to a most brilliant assembly indeed. They expressed great approbation and some, I think, begin to feel. Good Lady Huntingdon is indeed a mother in Israel. She is all in a flame for Jesus."[24]

In all these activities there were some successes among fellow nobles and political figures, but there was also ridicule. When an aristocratic woman at court was asked where the countess was she responded sneeringly, "I suppose praying with her beggars."[25] The most scathing condemnation came from the Duchess of Buckingham, who having been invited by the countess to hear one of her preachers instead denounced Methodism:

> Their doctrines are most repulsive and strongly tinctured with impertinence and disrespect towards their superiors, in perpetually endeavoring to level all ranks, and do away with all distinctions. It is monstrous to be told that you have a heart as sinful as the common wretches that crawl on the earth. This is highly offensive and insulting; and I cannot but wonder that your Ladyship should relish any sentiments so much at variance with high rank and good breeding.[26]

A different response to her drawing room evangelism came from one of the most famous man of letters and cynics of the day, the fourth Earl of Chesterfield. As opposed to the Duchess of Buckingham, Chesterfield liked to talk about Christianity, as many dabblers in religion do; in the words of William Law, they are those for whom "religion lives only in their head, but something else has possession of their heart."[27] People like the duchess and the earl were happy for the church to remain as it was so that their privileged world would remain as it was.

24. Ibid., ii., 202.
25. Ibid., i., 175.
26. Ibid., i., 27.
27. Law, *Serious Call*, 59.

Her drawing room ministry continued for several years, until in 1751 for health reasons Selina Hastings moved to just outside Bristol. Here's a reminder that calling needs to be understood as dynamic rather than static. She wrote Charles Wesley soon after her move that for the past two years she had been unclear regarding her lifework. And so she waited. But this was active waiting: In 1756 she created a small group of believing women who lived with her. Upon meeting her in 1759 the Methodist vicar John Fletcher described her as "a modern prodigy, a Countess humble and pious."[28] Her letters reveal a woman theologically well read and astute, and that she was using her residential group to refine her sense of calling.

The problem with the attempts of the countess and others to revive the Anglican Church was that most clergy and bishops were less interested in renewal than order and their own well-being. Hence Methodists were refused ordination, purged from their parishes, and forced to preach outdoors—on street corners, in fields, at the entrance to coal mines—which further scandalized those in authority and nearly everyone else. Recognizing the situation, the countess began providing these men her own homes and, subsequently, created chapels as alternative venues. Legally as an earl's widow she could appoint up to two personal chaplains. Not only did she exceed this number but bent both law and custom by leasing and converting buildings, terming them her private chapels, recruiting and then reimbursing her chaplains to preach there. In her mind dwelling from time to time in such buildings or others attached to them met the legal definition of living quarters, whose "private" chapels were exempt from the local bishop's control. Inviting relatives, friends, friends of friends, and anyone else to attend such services clearly violated the spirit of British law. Creative ministry it might have been, but was it right?

She developed a core group of about twenty ministers she called on to preach for her, including Whitefield, the Wesleys, and a dozen or so younger men who served as itinerant preachers sent to where they were requested by locals. This was later expressed in a larger vision, the means to the end—which was renewal. Writing in 1773, the countess now expressed her lifework as "to sound a General & Universal claim over England, in the fields & Citys where the gospel has not yet been sounded. I see daily our work is more & more universal."[29] Apparently even this was insufficient, for

28. Seymour, *Huntingdon*, ii., 232.
29. Harding, *Countess of Huntingdon's Connexion*, 66.

five years later at age seventy-one she declared her goal was "the conversion of the world."[30]

This then was the initial stage of her calling, which might be labeled discernment through experimentation. She expressed her gift of organization, first experienced in running her family estates, but now in religious work, combining waiting with moving out in faith. She sought to minister to all the thirsty, from aristocrats to the middle classes and the poor, by gathering and working alongside a remarkable collection of men and women. And because she had come to understand that the source of living water was in her she grew in confidence in own spiritual authority over ordained and other men.

Achievements

The countess of Huntingdon was remarkably responsive to opportunities and creative in how her calling might be manifested. Using borrowed money and funds raised by selling her jewelry, in 1761 she opened the first of her chapels in Brighton, with many more to follow in the next two decades, whose purpose was to supplement the parish church by worship services at alternative times and on days other than Sunday. The countess would build, buy or lease a building, attach a personal residence to it, appoint a personal chaplain and then open the doors to all comers. In other cases she responded with financial support to locally generated requests for chapels. From the mountains of Wales to Westminster in London's West End, she created a system of chapels that by their music and preaching drew mainly workers and the lower middle class to them.

Along with other religious entrepreneurs who created chapels the countess understood the importance of what Methodists called "societies," cell groups where the faithful might be strengthened outside attendance at regular Sunday worship. Members prayed, sang, and shared spiritual experiences. In her words: "Preaching they may hear and yet be miserably ignorant, whereas prayer meetings must bring them on in the examination of the heart."[31] The chapel, then, was the physical opportunity for the society—the church—to gather. And it existed not just for the members of the society. Many of her chapels had attached schools for poor children.

---

30. Seymour, *Huntingdon*, ii., 182.
31. Ibid., ii., 169.

Showing up at the services of one of the countess's chapels gave others an opportunity to donate money to the impoverished.

The chapels put her in contact with individuals across the country, providing opportunities to become an exhorter, encourager, teacher, and patron. From our vantage point perhaps her most unexpected role was as a mentor of men. Plenty of prominent spiritual leaders bared their souls to her, including Henry Venn, later curate of Clapham; John Fletcher, who asked if he should accept the offer of a new pastorate and sought her solace when spiritually discouraged; and of course Whitefield and the Wesley brothers, who with other leaders esteemed her godly character, theological acumen, and commitment to pray for them. She gave consolation to the disheartened among the more humble, including a dying soldier's wife, a blacksmith, and students. Her employment of such spiritual gifts reminded Whitefield of an ecclesiastic: "For a day or two she has had five clergymen under her roof, which makes her ladyship look *like a good archbishop, with his chaplains around him.*"[32]

Her role as patron extended well beyond her comfort zone. Although not personally opposed to slavery—by the time of her death significant public opposition to slavery still lay in the future—the countess sponsored and encouraged black authors such as the poet Phillis Wheatley and the anti-slavery activist Olaudah Equiano. Surely this sent a powerful message to her contemporaries, who, like the countess, were not yet convicted that slavery was incompatible with the Christian story.

One special group of men the countess mentored were the students at Trevecca College, which she founded in 1768 as the first institution of its kind, an "Academy for preachers."[33] Two of the "Oxford Seven" ended up at Trevecca, as did other young men recommended by sympathetic clergy and laypersons such as Viscountess Glenorchy, a Scots Presbyterian and recent convert. In a remodeled farmhouse walking distance from Howell Harris's Christian community in south Wales, in poor health and aged sixty the countess founded an alternative to Oxford and Cambridge for training Anglican clergy, which took form as a "School of the Prophets."[34] Calling Trevecca a "college" and having the students wear black gowns set a high standard; in some ways its opening was Methodism's academic coming of age.

32. Ibid., ii., 163.
33. Tyson, "Lady Huntington's Reformation," 589.
34. Seymour, *Huntingdon*, ii., 517.

But Trevecca was not intended to produce scholars or as a venue for discovering one's calling. Rather, the called showed up and were trained in the art of preaching by listening to some of the outstanding preachers of the time or practicing sermons before each other—beginning at 6 a.m. The countess supplied or raised support for the college (expending half her yearly income), for there was to be no charge for students, who were provided a stipend, room and board, books, clothing, and a horse. She personally examined applicants, whose qualification was that they had experienced the new birth; she also personally arranged pulpit engagements for them each weekend.

The ten to two dozen students at Trevecca in any given year studied Latin, Greek, and theology, but their focus was on learning to preach and then being sent out to do it. The students were generally penniless; the earliest class included a coal miner and an apprentice cabinet-maker. One of the original students later recalled how profoundly the college led to his sense of pardon for sin and personal knowledge of the truth.

When she was present at Trevecca, which was often for six months out of the year, the countess expounded scripture to students and prayed with and counseled them; one year she managed the college in the absence of a president. Although she once referred to herself as the students' "directress,"[35] Selina Hastings never felt called to preach—both her private personality and reading of scripture militated against this—although she told a female Quaker who she heard preach that "God who gives the rule can make the exception."[36] Rather, she understood her role to be an encourager of holiness and prayer. Thus it was that when Henry Venn spent three days at Trevecca he wrote, "Of all the people I ever saw, this society seems to me the most advanced in grace."[37]

The original plan was for students to stay at the college for three years, but many left to go into ministry before that. On some occasions the countess encouraged them in that direction—in one instance putting the Bible into the hand of a reluctant student who had never preached publicly, telling him to tell his audience either he was afraid of trusting God or to do the best he could and then pushing him out the door with the blessing, "The Lord be with you; do the best you can."[38] In sending two Trevecca students

---

35. Harding, *Countess of Huntingdon's Connexion*, 278.

36. Welch, *Spiritual Pilgrim*, 99.

37. Seymour, *Huntingdon*, ii., 482.

38. Ibid., ii., 126.

to Somersetshire she told them: "Come, come Meyer; come Seymour, you are only going to a few simple souls; tell them concerning Jesus Christ, and they will be satisfied."[39] She understood such souls, more than anything else, were thirsty.

Her itinerating students deepened the resentment of the establishment. Having sent two students on a preaching tour of the Kent coast the countess received a ferocious communication from one local curate: "Pray who gave you leave to send your preaching fellows into my parish? I desire you will command them to withdraw from Deal forthwith . . . I had enough of this business when your favourite Whitefield preached here many years ago, and I will not suffer a repetition of the same."[40] Such an attitude failed to account for why his parishioners showed up to hear mere students preach when their oratorical skills were likely less developed than his.

That it only existed in the years 1768–91, training a total of just 212 men, are less significant details than what those who attended went on to accomplish. Trevecca graduates became some of the more significant ministers in the late eighteenth and early nineteenth centuries: Jehoiada Brewer pastored large churches in the industrial cities of Sheffield and Birmingham, and John Johnson likewise in Manchester. Anthoy Crole led a Congregational church in London for twenty-six years, while John Johnson served a Presbyterian church in Edinburgh for fifty-eight years. Matthew Wilks succeeded George Whitefield in his two London pulpits, serving for more than half a century.

Trevecca provided not only preachers but missionaries. In this sense one might understand Selina Hastings's worldview as thinking locally, and then trying to act globally. Her first foray into missions came when Bethesda Orphan House in Georgia, founded by Whitefield, was bequeathed to the countess in 1770 after his death. She was then sixty-three and lived three thousand miles away. Having sunk huge sums into the orphanage a fire, the American Revolution (which she supported), and an administrator who turned out to be a something of a scoundrel sunk her ambitious plans for the institution to become a college. In the end Bethesda came into the hands of the state of Georgia. Like all risk-takers, her work comprised both successes and failures. Experiencing the latter did not blunt her zeal for globalizing the gospel.

---

39. Schlenther, *Huntingdon*, 146.

40. Seymour, *Huntingdon*, ii., 133.

Missionaries the countess encouraged and funded set out for the East Indies, Nova Scotia, and the South Pacific. One black Trevecca student went to America, and there were discussions about the French Revolution providing an opportunity to evangelize Paris. One mission to west Africa continues to bear fruit: in the early twenty-first century there are twenty-seven Countess of Huntingdon's Connexion churches in Sierra Leone.

In 1782 the countess began a correspondence with George Washington, a distant cousin, to found a college in America to provide spiritually for native Americans. She offered to name the general as one of her executors for her American property, and in 1784 sent him a six-page *Address to America* outlining her plans, which included several American states donating land to the project. In return she would "transfer both my trust estate with all my own property in Georgia."[41] But while Patrick Henry, the Governor of Virginia, presented the plans to Congress he privately informed Washington, and the president in turn wrote the countess, that the plan was financially and politically impossible—although she was still at work on the project up until her death in 1791.

Clearly, leadership was an important piece of her calling, evident as early as her management of her husband's lands and households. Subsequently Whitefield asked her to manage his congregations, recognizing he did not have the gift of administration, writing to her, "a leader is wanting. This honour hath been put upon your Ladyship by the great head of the church."[42] Until she was eighty the countess moved around the kingdom in order to manage her chapels and Trevecca College, in an age when travelling was difficult even for the young and fit.

The Countess of Huntingdon was a pragmatist regarding the Church of England, wishing to remain in and reform the church, but willing to bend or break its rules. She gathered believers into societies, called and sent out pastors, and funded the network of chapels that came to be known as Countess of Huntingdon's Connexion. Use of the possessive is important, but nevertheless until 1783 it was her intention to revive not separate from Church of England. Her Connexion's chapels used Anglican liturgy, the Prayer Book, the creed, and hymns of the Church.

Then in the late 1770s crisis came. The Spa Fields Chapel in north London, which she leased, remodeled, and attached a living quarters to, was the flagship society of the Connexion, with its own charity school and

41. Ibid., ii., 274.
42. Ibid., ii., 117.

extensive financial support of other chapels. William Sellon, the Anglican curate in whose parish the building was situated, jealous and furious that the chapel was depriving him of income, brought legal action, claiming his right to preach at Spa Fields whenever he wished, to determine who else might preach there, and to be paid for both. There were numerous attempts at compromise, but the avaricious Sellon was inflexible. Having lost the legal battle the countess was left with no alternative except to leave the Church of England and establish a separate denomination. Sellon had forced a choice that had been in the background for decades, in this instance between breaking church rules and submitting to his depredations. In a letter to the Archbishop of Canterbury Hastings lamented being driven "by painful necessity from the Communion of the established Church,"[43] although in their minds her ministers would remain true to the Anglican Church, "maintain[ing] her Doctrines, though we cannot in all things submit to her Discipline."[44]

Spa Fields Chapel, something of a model for the modern megachurch, offers important insights into the operation of the Connexion's congregations. Lay leadership was emphasized. Although the countess ran a tight ship, decision-making was democratic, and leaders disagreed with her on a variety of matters, e.g., that a minister she had recruited was in their words "no doubt an honest and gracious soul, but is not adapted for this place."[45] While authoritarian, the countess produced independence in others, and provided for a collective succession to her leadership of the Connexion, calling men "to unite for the Carring the Gospel forward abroad and at Home and to put it into such a line of General usefullness that when the Lord Calls for me my absence will not make more than an old shoe Cast aside."[46]

Although she founded a new denomination, Selina Hastings believed the church to be one body. It is fair to say the division between John Wesley and the countess was as much about personality as belief. While fundamental questions divided Methodists—critically, how much free will did people have in light of God's sovereignty—as the countess put it regarding Christian work, "I wish all success, though they gather not with me."[47]

43. Welch, "Lady Huntingdon and Spa Fields Chapel," 181.

44. Seymour, *Huntingdon*, ii., 313.

45. Welch, *Two Methodist Chapels*, 58.

46. Welch, *Spiritual Pilgrim*, 207.

47. Seymour, *Huntingdon*, ii., 420.

When John Wesley was seriously ill in 1775 she wrote his brother: "How does one hour of loving sorrow swallow up the just differences our various judgments make . . . I have loved him this five and thirty years and it is with pleasure I find he remains in my heart as a friend and a laborious beloved servant of Jesus Christ."[48]

By the time she died at age eighty-three the Countess of Huntingdon had founded, helped to build, or had become the patron for sixty-four chapels. She directed and helped finance the preaching circuits of sixty ministers; she funded hundreds of students at Trevecca. She had helped write a creed and assemble a hymnal for her Connexion. Through her network of chaplains she quietly distributed to charities what would be today millions of dollars. Her charitable rule derived from her reading of William Law's book: "When I gave myself up to the Lord, I likewise devoted to him all my fortune."[49] Her pragmatic philosophy of giving was based on the simple yet profound question, Where can I make a difference? She suggested as an answer that, "There were many benevolent persons who had no religion, who would feel for the temporal distress of others, and help them; but few, even among the religious, who had a proper concern for the awful condition of ignorant and perishing souls."[50] To carry out her work she expended her personal fortune, used rents from both land and houses, the American property inherited from Whitefield, contributions and loans from others, and sale of her jewels, silver plate, and investments.

Just before she died she noted that "The Lord hath been present with my spirit this morning in a remarkable manner: what he means to convey to my mind I know not; it may be my approaching departure; my soul is filled with glory; I am as in the element of heaven itself."[51] Her last act in life was to secure the services of a minister for the Spa Fields Chapel, and when told he had accepted she passed away—reminiscent of another complicated personality: "When David had served God's purpose in his own generation, he fell asleep" (Acts 13:36). Selina Hastings died as she had lived since her conversion: by her request she was buried privately in an unmarked grave beside her husband. Breaking with the revenge theme of her family of origin she left sizeable bequests to her estranged daughter, her grandson (who when he came of age received all her landed estates), and with what was left

---

48. Cook, *Countess of Huntingdon*, 352.

49. Seymour, *Huntingdon*, ii., 518.

50. Ibid.

51. Tyson and Schlenther, *Early Methodism*, 294–95.

provided for her sixty-four chapels. Her legacies include a denomination of some 120 congregations with its own theological college, now absorbed into Westminster College, Cambridge University; the Bethesda Home for Boys, Savannah, Georgia; and the Connexion churches in west Africa. Her efforts enriched the soil of the Church of England and other Protestants, including the Presbyterian Church of Wales, Baptists and Congregationalists in England, as well as Methodists and Moravians.

But all these accomplishments are externalities. The *progress* of her life is what provides a template for us, and allows us to pay less heed to her shortcomings—which were numerous: she had a quick temper; was strong-willed, even authoritarian; at times she could be unforgiving and on other occasions easily misled regarding the character of her associates; she was impetuous. Her strong sense of calling rubbed some souls the wrong way. She should have delegated more. As an activist she felt free to order the lives of her ministers, students, church committees, and when she could bishops and politicians, although not for personal power. But she also apologized, forgave, repented divisions with other believers, consoled the young Trevecca students when they confessed they were not up to the task, and contributed to the work of men with whom she had earlier broken ties. One congregation always wrote to her as Mother Huntingdon, while a student called her "my best earthly friend,"[52] suggesting a sweetness of character at odds with typical domineering personalities.

The story of Selina Hastings reveals how one individual could make a mark on her times. Although she published almost nothing and sought to have nothing published about her, what's clear is that men whose education far surpassed hers, ministers included, deferred to her, and not merely because she was wealthy. They sensed her discernment, particularly on doctrinal issues. They experienced her generosity, and they saw her courage in overcoming personal circumstances—that she did not grow weary and lose heart. These made up for her deficiencies because contemporaries realized how vital her role was in the new reformation happening around them. Might this mean that godliness trumped gender prejudice in the eighteenth century? If so the history of those times needs revision.

She left debts of £3,000, a very large figure at the time, mostly from costs associated with a chapel she had just purchased in London; her executors had to sell her several homes to pay the debt off. Cardinal Newman, overlooking her theology, concluded that "she did not allow the homage

---

52. Seymour, *Huntingdon*, ii., 303–4.

due to her rank to remain with herself: she . . . offered them up to Christ. She acted as one ought to act who considered this life a pilgrimage, not a home."[53] An aristocrat unafraid to cross class divisions, hers is a case of triumph over disabilities like poor health. After her death one of her ministers wrote that, "she was far from a perfect character, yet I hesitate not to say that among the illustrious and noble of the country she has not left her equal."[54]

And so to return to the question with which this chapter began, "What is the church?" Regarding Selina Hastings, Countess of Huntingdon, she waited until the Church of England had made her situation intolerable and, then in her words, she was "cast out of the Church now only for what I have been doing this forty years—speaking and living for Jesus Christ."[55] Thereupon though a female layperson she created a network of believers both of and separate from the Church of England. That's her message to us. She persisted in spite of struggles, standing her ground but open to the Spirit finally saying, "it's over." In the end the Anglican authorities made her the world's first Methodist.

Her Text

You wish for my advice relative to the Ministry. From the connection you stand in with me, you have a just right to claim, not only my wishes and prayers for you, but the long experience of a poor, unprofitable servant, now near fifty years facing hell and the world, in my most dear and divine Master Jesus Christ's service; . . .

Two points I must lay down as most indispensable qualifications for a Minister of the Everlasting Gospel. The first is, The invariable conviction that the Church of Christ can have no establishment upon earth, but that which came down from Heaven on the day of Pentecost, and which is continued to it. From thence only *all truth* can be derived; all else must be of the world, as having no better origin; and what does not come down from Heaven, can have no property that can cause its return thither. This is the true church of Christ only, under all denominations upon earth. Modes, manners, and political governments of all kinds, prove but the distress of the times, from our ignorance, carnality, and unbelief in the Son of God.

53. Newman, "Selina, Countess of Huntingdon," 387–88.
54. Cook, *Countess of Huntingdon*, 422.
55. Tyson and Schlenther, *Early Methodism*, 15.

Take so many dead men, and dress them in their coffins, in the habit of each profession of religion upon earth, they are still but dead bodies; you see all they are: Such only is the church, the people, or individuals, that are not of that Jerusalem from above. Look, then, to that call which is to *that* Church. *This true church* has nothing but *faith to live* upon: as it belongs not to this world, it cannot even rationally be supposed to find any thing here of its own nature to continue life to it; therefore, it cannot exist without *faith*, which is the gift of God.

This, then, must be the second point to be insisted on, to prove your ministry fruitful. . . . O that he may give you that powerful faith that overcomes the sinners heart! and though hell should rise in judgment against you, *One*, above all, shall say, "Well done, good and faithful servant." . . . Vanity, that worst of all evils (which ignorance only supposes wisdom in man to direct his ways), falls in love with itself, and forever excludes all divine teachings from heaven, which never were, nor ever will be known but by the poor in spirit, to whom the kingdom of God expressly belongs.

Copy of a Letter from the Countess of Huntingdon to One of Her Students (1785)

Questions

1. To what extent does the life of the Countess of Huntingdon help us understand the religious revival in the eighteenth-century English-speaking world?

2. What do you think about her response to what she understood her calling to be after her husband died?

3. Concerning the debate among the Methodist reformers over faith versus works, what do you think? Does your thinking fan the flame of your faith or quench your thirst?

4. What should she have done regarding Spa Fields, when the rules of the Church she loved were being used against her? Was her previous skirting the edge of the law justified? How are we to understand the importance of adhering to rules?

5. Ask the question she asked: Where can I make a difference? Write the answer here:

_____.

For Further Reading

Cook, Faith. *Selina, Countess of Huntingdon*. Carlisle: Banner of Truth Trust, 2001.

Harding Alan. *The Countess of Huntingdon's Connexion: A Sect in Action in Eighteenth-Century England*. Oxford: Oxford University Press, 2003.

Kirby, Gilbert, *The Elect Lady*. (1972; 1990) Online: http://homepage.ntlworld.com/ben. quant/connexions/electlady.html.

Welch, Edwin. *Spiritual Pilgrim: A Reassessment of the Life of the Countess of Huntingdon*. Cardiff: University of Wales Press, 1995.

CHAPTER 2

Olaudah Equiano

Story: Identity—Who am I?

> I offer here the history of neither a saint, a hero, nor a tyrant.
> Olaudah Equiano, aged 44

"I WISH TO STAND by my own integrity."[1] These are the words of one of the most remarkable individuals I've ever run across. His story speaks to all of us whose aspirations have been unfairly frustrated by others, who are not yet free to pursue their dreams, but who in not giving up model the virtue of fortitude. And because some dreams are not worth pursuing, discernment is another vital element revealed by the subject of this chapter.

Sometime around 1745 Olaudah Equiano was born in the southeast region of what is now the African nation of Nigeria. During the next five decades he was to travel, at first involuntarily as a slave, to the African coast, and from there to the Caribbean, several North American colonies, London, the Arctic, and finally throughout the British Isles. Concurrently, his name changed several times, as did his religious beliefs and sense of purpose. From the degradation of being another man's property, by the time of his death Equiano had become the wealthiest and most famous black person in Britain, and very much a public figure. But that was not his identity—that was not who he was.

1. Equiano, *Narrative*, 190.

Having left his homeland in the 1750s, never to return, in time Equiano became, in his words, "the African." His life work was to speak for the millions of sons and daughters of Africa sold into slavery, many of whom perished during the infamous Middle Passage between Africa and the Americas, others brutally exploited on plantations in the Caribbean islands or mainland British colonies. When Equiano died in 1797 they were not yet free, nor had human trafficking ended. But the conversation he energized was to continue until international debate ended first the slave trade, then slavery itself in the European empires, and finally in the United States. Although an audacious claim, it could be argued that because Equiano became a believer the enslavement of Africans by Europeans came to an end.

According to his 1789 autobiography, *The Interesting Narrative of the Life of Olaudah Equiano*, written when he was in his forties, Equiano was born in an Igbo village in the west African interior. Identity in his case was constructed on a foundation of strong family bonds, sense of place and his future there, and an understanding of the Igbo concept of *chi*, the notion that an individual god, something like a guardian angel, had written a script for your life. But then as a boy aged somewhere around eleven he and his sister were kidnapped by raiders from a neighboring clan, who sold them into slavery. From a member of a tightly-knit community he became a commodity. Equiano was then resold and renamed several times as he was moved to the coast of Africa, and from there transported first to Barbados—a trip normally taking two months—and then to the Virginia colony. Helpless and terrified on the voyage, he was unable to make sense of how the ship moved or who the European sailors were. Seeing blacks brutalized and a white sailor flogged to death and his body dumped overboard, the horror of this experience can be understood in reading his own words: "I expected they would sacrifice me."[2]

In Virginia he had the good fortune to be purchased by a British navy officer, Michael Henry Pascal, who introduced him to a life of sea-going, thus providing a set of alternatives rarely experienced by the millions of slaves who lived and died on plantations in the New World. His new master named him Gustavus Vassa, after the Swedish noble who two centuries earlier led his nation's fight for freedom against Denmark; a popular play on the subject was currently on the London stage. Although it appears Pascal intended the name as a joke, it turned out to be a doubly remarkable choice: Equiano had been the son of a village notable, and later in Britain he would

2. Ibid., 55.

play a crucial role in the opposition to the slave trade—the first step in freeing his people. And to make matters even more fascinating Olaudah Equiano's Igbo first name meant "vicissitude or fortune," or "one favored" and "well-spoken." We will return to the significance of his African name on several occasions. For now we get some insight into what names represented for Equiano because he at first refused to accept the new designation and had to be beaten into submission. But he took on "Gustavus Vassa" and was to call himself publicly by that name during the rest of his life, whereas "Olaudah Equiano" was the first name that appears on the title page of his autobiography, a name he rarely used previously. And so we may ask, what do our names mean to us?

As Equiano acknowledged he was now Vassa, so did he not so much fight against his slave status—his new identity—as he discovered how to exploit it. Combined with fundamental personality traits—an innate curiosity about past, present, and future, a remarkable intellect, and an entrepreneurial spirit, longing even at age seventeen to work for himself—his situation on board Pascal's ship brought the young slave invaluable experience. In spite of the irony that Britain exploited enslaved men to defend the nation's freedom, Vassa used the opportunity provided by the wooden walls of the Royal Navy to become a skilled seaman, and in the process learned English, mathematics, the art of navigation, and several trades. Simultaneously, he explored and experienced vast oceans and several continents, engaged in commerce throughout the Atlantic world, and was introduced to the Bible.

As advantageous as his position in the meritocratic British navy was compared to the life of most enslaved Africans, the color of his skin and his position as a slave also meant repeated experiences of terror and humiliation. Sailing with his owner in the Atlantic and Mediterranean, at one point he was told by crew members that he would be killed and eaten. It is no wonder, then, that Equiano's autobiography is filled with references to despair, psychological depression, and six distinct passages where he expressed thoughts of suicide.

But if mistreatment might shatter one's sense of self, betrayal is worse. What Vassa thought was a father/son relationship with his master, as well as what he had come to expect as a reward for his faithful service in the British navy during the Seven Years' War against France, proved ill-founded. Although Captain Pascal had never promised Vassa his freedom he usually treated him kindly and had impressed on the young slave the importance of living morally as a means of earning God's love. Poor theology reflected a deeper delusion.

The expectations of a young man now in his late teens were dashed when Pascal not only sold him to a slave trader bound for the Caribbean, threatening to cut Vassa's throat if he failed to comply, but refused to provide Vassa a share of the wartime prize money rightfully due him as a member of a ship's crew that had captured several enemy vessels. As a sign of his pluck, even as a teenager, in that moment of deep discouragement Vassa had the courage to speak to his subsequent owner against this unfairness: "I have been baptized, and by the laws of the land no man has a right to sell me."[3]

In his early teens while in London with Pascal visiting the officer's cousins Vassa had agreed to be baptized, perhaps to ingratiate him with the family or, given his response at the moment of betrayal, because he trusted that combined with this action British law would offer protection and confer equality. He was to learn baptism did not make him a Christian and that while in his mind he was now more European than African the law was ineffectual in light of pervasive racism and exploitation. In the end he came to believe that only he could make himself free. But he retained his African understanding of destiny, commenting in the context of this disappointment that, "As I was from early years a predestinarian, I thought whatever fate had determined for me must come to pass; and therefore, if it were my lot to be free nothing could prevent me . . . [O]n the other hand, if it were my fate not to be freed I never should be so."[4] How this understanding worked out in his life reveals Equiano beginning to think Christianly— examining his behavior, wondering if Pascal's act of betrayal was a "judgment of Heaven."[5] He "acknowledged my transgression to God, and poured out my soul before him with unfeigned repentance."[6] And while several times considering running away he chose to serve his masters loyally while at the same time engaging in trade so as to earn enough money to purchase his freedom.

And so Vassa was sold again, eventually becoming the property of Robert King, a Quaker merchant from Philadelphia who, based on the West Indian island of Montserrat, traded across the Caribbean and with

3. Ibid., 85.

4. Ibid., 105.

5. Ibid., 86.

6. Ibid.

several North American colonies. His latest master wisely understood Vassa's value, not only as a skilled sailor but as a quick-witted, literate, and entrepreneurial individual. Vassa labored in every aspect of King's business network, including on board his master's numerous ships.

At the same time he was, in his words, "a witness to cruelties of every kind,"[7] from the rape of young female slaves and the mutilation and burning alive of male slaves to the re-enslavement of free blacks. Vassa was robbed and defrauded over and over again by dishonest white seamen and traders; in Savannah he was so badly beaten by a drunken doctor and his accomplice that he was unable to get out of bed for three weeks. In contrast to eighteenth-century rhetoric, as readers encounter these episodes through Vassa's experiences the identity of the true savages dawns on us.

In spite of these ordeals, or perhaps because of them, Vassa continued to save money from his trading until he was able to purchase his freedom. On July 10, 1766, in his early twenties and after having been a slave for a decade, he became "my own master, and completely free. I thought this was the happiest day I had ever experienced."[8] While intending to return to England, curiously he remained for a year in the West Indies. Vassa knew from observation that to be a free black person in the slave societies of North America and the Caribbean, even when one could produce documentation proving free status, was always to face the threat of being exploited, physically abused or even kidnapped and sold. Color trumped character in the minds of many, as he was to experience again. But sometimes character won out: on one occasion when his captain died on the voyage and the mate was ill, Vassa brought the ship into port. "I now obtained a new appellation, and was called Captain. This elated me not a little, and it was quite flattering to my vanity."[9]

Part of the fascination with his autobiography is that it reads like an adventure novel. Equiano's *Narrative* was brilliantly written and, understandably, a best-seller for years after it was first published. It is part autobiography of a remarkable person, part travelogue of strange and wonderful places—from Africa to the West Indies, from Savannah, Georgia to Smyrna, Turkey. The narrator observed a profusely sweating George Whitefield preaching in Georgia, a young Horatio Nelson, and James Wolfe just before that general's heroic death in the battle of Quebec. He was shipwrecked on

7. Ibid., 97.
8. Ibid., 120.
9. Ibid., 125.

several occasions and icebound in the Arctic while a member of a 1773 expedition seeking the Northwest Passage. But another way to read the *Narrative* is to see these and other episodes through Equiano's eyes as moments of recognition—God sightings we might say—and as opportunities for self-transformation, turning points on the road to freedom: Equiano's, to be certain, but on the largest stage for millions of slaves.

In some ways then he was the most modern of men. Equiano tells us "almost every event of my life made an impression on my mind, and influenced my conduct. I early accustomed myself to look at the hand of God in the minutest occurrence, and to learn from it a lesson of morality and religion."[10] Yet he would have found curious the hyper-individualism so characteristic of modern times. In the *Narrative* he commented on numerous occasions that what was happening to him was also happening in the lives of all slaves and free black people. Therefore, his life was to be understood as a representation of something much larger than one man's experience: his autobiography was their history.

As Equiano explored the North Sea, Atlantic, Caribbean, and Mediterranean he also investigated different spiritualities. His study of the Bible revealed the "laws and rules of my own country written almost exactly here,"[11] which aided his remembering what his west African homeland was like decades after he left it, but allowed him to look forward as well: as he walked to the government office on Montserrat to get his manumission papers his mind went to Psalm 126, with its lines, "May those who sow in tears reap with shouts of joy" (Ps 126:5). Equiano discussed theology with a Catholic priest in Spain, observed Quaker and Jewish meetings, attended Anglican services, and pondered why Turkish Muslims often seemed more moral than Christians in Europe and the Americas; indeed, at one point he tried to join the crew of a ship bound for Turkey, "there to end my days."[12]

But even in the face of his past experiences in the West Indies, he kept returning there and signing on with ships' captains despite his familiarity with the unethical dealings of such men. Was it the triumph of hope over experience—that on shipboard it ought to be what you could do not what class or color you were? Was it his love of travel? Or was it his sense of identity—a sea-faring entrepreneur is who he thought he was, that is, he never accepted that he was a slave or that as a free man that the color of

10. Ibid., 195–96.
11. Ibid., 83.
12. Ibid., 151.

his skin should confer status? To answer these questions we need to circle back to understand how Equiano worked through his identity up to one fateful day in 1774 when he experienced an encounter that changed his life forever.

Memory is an important tool for answering the question, "Who am I?" For Equiano, recall allowed him to balance his emerging identities. Throughout the *Narrative* the reader encounters the phrase, "I remember," at first applied to his childhood, but then to biblical verses as framing his experiences. In the process this transformed his sense of self from Igbo to "a son of Africa" who was also British. Thus he commented that from the age of fourteen he saw European society as in some ways superior to what he recalled from his African home. But he also made informed judgments regarding some Europeans. In his mind, the biblical story was universal rather than European. This made arguments based on biblical texts justifying enslavement of Africans by Europeans, which apologists for slavery frequently employed, all the more perverse. Whereas he first "embraced every occasion of improvement, and every new thing that I observed I treasured up in my memory,"[13] he ended up preaching the golden rule to proslavery Europeans: "O, ye nominal Christians! Might not an African ask you, learned you this from your God, who says unto you, Do unto all men as you would men should do unto you."[14]

On the one hand, this combination of African, British, and emerging Christian identities allowed him to cease being frightened by abusive whites—and thus he speaks to all people who are prone to fear their oppressors. On the other he publicized the true identity of those oppressors as nominal or false Christians because they did what God would not, placing shackles on other humans, and thus had behaved as if they were greater than God.

Equiano also came to understand himself as a man of action, who despite being a slave took charge in dangerous shipboard situations when his white fellow sailors or superiors panicked. The downside to this part of his personality was that spiritually this took form as a high degree of self-righteousness. Equiano continually compared himself to others using the Ten Commandments as a yardstick. He was the most righteous person he knew because he kept eight of the ten, struggling only with swearing and with observing the Sabbath—occupational hazards for sailors.

13. Ibid., 72.
14. Ibid., 58.

Every time he tried to go to Turkey someone frustrated his plans, which only made his swearing worse. He then experienced a vision of "the great and awful scene of the judgment day."[15] From this he asked God for forgiveness, and sensed "clearly what a bad use I had made of the faculties I was endowed with,"[16] but as well he pointed out to believing readers "I was still in nature's darkness."[17] He was drawn to read the Bible, and met an old sailor, now a silk weaver and more importantly a believer, who invited him to his church—which reminded Equiano of what he had read in the Bible about the early Christians. Yet among them for two months he was offended by being told that keeping eight of the Ten Commandments was insufficient, that he needed to repent for his sins, experience new birth and know those sins had been forgiven. Now unemployed and vexed about who he was in the scale of eternity, he signed on as steward on a ship, the *Hope*, bound for Cadiz, Spain. One could do much worse than joining some entity named Hope.

Conversion

If leaving Africa as a boy was one memorable turning point in his life, his conversion experience when he was around age thirty was another. It is best to understand this moment in his words, but also in its context. Two important factors frame what was about to happen. As we have already seen, long before his conversion Equiano had a strong sense of providence, "a *particular favorite of heaven*"[18] he called himself, as his parents had named him Olaudah, "one favored." Likewise, he observed and experienced important dreams—of a shipmate warned in a dream to leave his berth prior to a collision, before meeting a fortune teller in Philadelphia who predicted future tight spots he would be in as well as his eventual freedom, and dreams three nights in a row on board a ship before a wreck caused by an incompetent captain. Where do dreams come from? Were Christian shipmates praying for him, because perhaps that is part of why dreams of God come to those who do not yet believe?

And so Equiano tells us that all during the day of October 6, 1774 "I thought that I should either see or hear something supernatural. I had

15. Ibid., 152.
16. Ibid., 153.
17. Ibid.
18. Ibid., 33.

a secret impulse on my mind of something that was to take place, which drove me continually for that time to a throne of grace. It pleased God to enable me to wrestle with him, as Jacob did: I prayed that if sudden death were to happen, and I perished, it might be at Christ's feet."[19] That evening he read and meditated on Acts 4:12: "There is salvation in no one else, for there is no other name under heaven given among mortals by which we must be saved." While at first he "began to think I had lived a moral life, and that I had a proper ground to believe I had an interest in the divine favor,"[20] he continued to be troubled, "not knowing whether salvation was to be had partly for our own good deeds, or solely as the sovereign gift of God."[21] At that moment "the Lord was pleased to break in upon my soul with his bright beams of heavenly light . . . I saw clearly, with the eye of faith, the crucified Savior bleeding on the cross on Mount Calvary: the Scriptures became an unsealed book . . . I saw the Lord Jesus Christ in his humiliation, loaded and bearing my reproach, sin, and shame. I then clearly perceived, that by the deeds of the law no flesh living could be justified."[22] Apparently 80 percent is not passing in some venues.

Salvation opened a window onto Equiano's past: "Now every leading providential circumstance that happened to me, from the day I was taken from my parents to that hour, was then, in my view, as if it had but just then occurred. I was sensible of the invisible hand of God, which guided and protected me when in truth I knew it not: still the Lord pursued me although I slighted and disregarded it; this mercy melted me down. . . . I wept, seeing what a great debtor I was to sovereign free grace."[23] These lines are reminiscent of others, for example in God telling Isaiah:

> I have redeemed you;
> I have summoned you by name; you are mine.
> When you pass through the waters,
> I will be with you;
> and when you pass through the rivers,
> they will not sweep over you.
> When you walk through the fire,
> you will not be burned;
> the flames will not set you ablaze. (Isa 43:1–2)

19. Ibid., 159.
20. Ibid.
21. Ibid.
22. Ibid.
23. Ibid., 160.

Salvation opened another window onto his present: "I felt an astonishing change; the burden of sin, the gaping jaws of hell, and the fears of death, that weighed me down before, now lost their horror."[24] And most importantly, there was still another window opened onto Equiano's future: "I felt a deep concern for my mother and friends, which occasioned me to pray with fresh ardor; and, in the abyss of thought, I viewed the unconverted people of the world in a very awful state, being without God and without hope."[25] On a ship named *Hope* he had acquired a deep faith that would allow him to love in ways never before possible.

Equiano's new identity produced the sort of joy that believers before and after would realize, a joy which nevertheless seems wacky to those who have yet to experience it: "It pleased God to pour out on me the spirit of prayer and the grace of supplication, so that in loud acclamations I was enabled to praise and glorify his most holy name. When I got out of the cabin, and told some of the people what the Lord had done for me, alas! who could understand me or believe my report!"[26] Let's be honest: such expression of elation would make most of us very uncomfortable. Equiano then continues: "I became a barbarian to them in talking of the love of Christ: his name was to me as ointment poured forth; indeed it was sweet to my soul, but to them a rock of offence. . . . I had uncommon commotions within."[27] Why is it that we can identify with joy expressed about trifles such as sports or movies but often feel discomfort with joy expressed about matters of eternal significance?

After years in which he had read the Word, the Word now read him: "Now the Bible was my only companion and comfort; I prized it much, with many thanks to God that I could read it for myself, and was not left to be tossed about or led by man's devices and notions. The worth of a soul cannot be told."[28] Through these words Equiano tells his readers that, unlike the cliché common today—knowledge is power—he understood that faith is power, because it provides the capacity to overcome culture, context, and circumstance. Not without reason, Equiano carried a copy of the Bible with him wherever he went.

24. Ibid.
25. Ibid.
26. Ibid.
27. Ibid.
28. Ibid.

Equiano then explained where this new capacity had taken him: "May the Lord give the reader an understanding in this. Whenever I looked into the Bible I saw things new, and many texts were immediately applied to me with great comfort, for I knew that to me was the word of salvation sent. Sure I was that the Spirit which [proclaimed] the word opened my heart to receive the truth of it as it is in Jesus—that the same Spirit enabled me to act in faith upon the promises which were precious to me, and enabled me to believe to the salvation of my soul."[29] Even as an enslaved boy he constantly asked people questions, trying to understand what new things he encountered were and how they worked. When he turned to the Bible and used same approach he found answers to who he was, to his true identity and subsequently his calling.

He who had for so long and in so many ways gone without liberty was now, at last, free. And so in the portrait Equiano had commissioned, which appeared as the frontispiece to his 1789 autobiography, he holds a Bible opened to Acts 4:12, offering it in turn to viewers, as if to ask, as he looks them in the eye, "Do you believe this?" Eight years after he purchased his freedom from Robert King he came to understand that his freedom had been purchased for him. Contemporaries would have understood the nature of the invitation. And because just a year earlier a horrific image of 294 Africans crammed into a slave ship was widely published we should not miss what else the portrait portrays to viewers: Equiano was not a commodity, but a human made in the image of God.

Olaudah Equiano

Calling

Equiano would eventually be able to define his identity as an African Christian called to live in a land of exile, never to return home, so that other Africans would never again be forced to leave their homes for a land of exile. But how did he come to this understanding?

Equiano became the most important Afro-British voice in the growing opposition in the 1780s to the slave trade, a movement which would have

29. Ibid., 160–61.

been unpredictable just a few years earlier. Were he merely a self promoter, Equiano's *Narrative* would have jumped from the story of his conversion to the consummation of his faith in the form of this new life project, omitting twists and turns—many of them wrong. But this is not the reality of the lives believers experience, and so in fact there follow several revealing and two embarrassing episodes he discusses in his autobiography.

Equiano foolishly agreed to go on one last voyage to the New World, in this case to Georgia. Along the way the ship was wrecked on some rocks. None of the white sailors, including the captain, proved capable of responding to the situation; it was Equiano who organized a response, and not a single person aboard the ship was lost. While in Georgia after befriending some whites they turned on him; other whites attempted to re-enslave Equiano and he was degraded in other ways. Several years later he made two additional voyages to the West Indies—"being still of a roving disposition"[30]—and again was cheated by scoundrels.

He returned to the West Indies one final time, to work for an old acquaintance and former employer, the celebrated inventor Dr. Charles Irving, in what appears to have been a get-rich-quick scheme to create a plantation on the Mosquito Coast in present-day Nicaragua. Equiano was to be an agent in choosing slaves and then act as their overseer on the plantation. He justified his acceptance of the position on the basis of his long relationship with Irving, perhaps another father figure, and the opportunity for evangelism: "I hoped to be an instrument, under God, of bringing some poor sinner to my well-beloved master, Jesus Christ."[31] Of course that master taught we cannot serve God and Mammon, and the project in the end was a complete failure. Convicted of his actions, Equiano recalled: "What does it avail a man if he gain the whole world and lose his soul?"[32]

Equiano then experienced extreme difficulties in returning from the plantation to London: he was nearly enslaved for a second time, and was brutalized, swindled and almost killed, which he discerned as God trying to get his attention. He had come to understand that as long as there existed a trade in slaves—and his own father had owned slaves—Africans would be exposed to abuse and indignities. Therefore the only solution was abolition. On this he never looked back.

30. Ibid., 144.
31. Ibid., 169.
32. Ibid., 175.

Achievements

In March 1789, in support of the abolitionist cause he had made his own, Equiano published his 530-page autobiography, *The Interesting Narrative of the Life of Olaudah Equiano*. He was the first ex-slave to tell the story of his African roots, kidnapping, the horror of traveling on a slave ship and the terrible experiences that followed. Overnight the *Narrative* became an essential text for British and American abolitionists, and remained so for the succeeding two generations, critically undermining the concept of Christian slaveholding as biblically defensible. Ponder just one passage in the *Narrative*:

> One Mr. Drummond told me that he had sold 41,000 Negroes, and that he once cut off a Negro man's leg for running away. I asked him if the man had died in the operation, how he, as a Christian, could answer for the horrid act before God? and he told me, answering was a thing of another world, what he thought and did were policy. I told him that the Christian doctrine taught us to do unto others as we would that others should do unto us. He then said that his scheme had the desired effect—it cured that man and some others of running away.[33]

Was there any reasonable answer to the question posed by the passage, other than condemning the inhumanity of men such as Drummond while challenging them to consider their understanding of the connection between this world and the one to come?

Elsewhere in his *Narrative*, speaking of slaves, Equiano asked the rhetorical question, "If these are not the poor, the broken-hearted, the blind, the captive, the bruised, which our Savior speaks of, who are they?"[34] In contrast with the rags-to-riches story in Benjamin Franklin's iconic *Autobiography*, Equiano's is more like what most of us experience: where might and right clash might frequently wins.

The *Narrative* and his other writings challenged Europeans on this moral issue. In reviewing a book published by a defender of slavery he urged reading Acts 17:26: "From one ancestor God made all nations." In warning that the image of Africans held by most Europeans at the time failed to conform to the ideal of Christian equality, he rallied many readers to the side of right. Thus in a 1791 letter to William Wilberforce, John

33. Ibid., 94.
34. Ibid., 97.

Wesley wrote as he lay dying: "Reading this morning a tract wrote by a poor African, I was particularly struck by the circumstance, that a man who has black skin, being wronged or outraged by a white man, can have no redress; it being a LAW in our Colonies that the OATH of a black man against a white goes for nothing. What villainy is this!"[35] Six weeks after the publication of Equiano's *Interesting Narrative*, Wilberforce introduced a bill in the House of Commons to abolish the slave trade.

What Wesley and Wilberforce understood was the powerful argument that Equiano was making, not for human rights in the abstract but on the basis of the practice of common decency that readers of the Bible should expect from one another. In other words, human rights had spiritual roots, and only that comprehension could confront everyday discrimination. It surely says something about our own times that, until late in the twentieth century, when abridgements of the *Interesting Narrative* were published the segment detailing Equiano's conversion was almost always left out.

It should be noted that Equiano self-published his *Interesting Narrative*. That is, he lined up at first hundreds and eventually thousands of subscribers who by ordering copies of a book not yet published provided Equiano the funds for printing his autobiography; these included the Countess of Huntington, who we have already observed, and Hannah More, who we are about to. When the *Interesting Narrative* quickly sold out Equiano, maintaining the copyright, brought out eight subsequent editions in the next five years and went off on promotional tours of England, Scotland, and Ireland. What had not changed from his days as a slave was Equiano's ingenuity and entrepreneurship.

Equiano created a four-fold identity for himself: black, British, Christian—and free. He freed himself, in the end choosing his identity rather than accepting what those who wished him ill had tried to impose. This identity was *within* a community of men and women of different backgrounds, because Equiano came to understand people first and foremost as individuals rather than merely members of nationalities. Whereas on earlier occasions he had hoped God would strike dead those who were oppressing him, two years after his conversion, while being tortured by a malevolent ship captain in the West Indies he "prayed to God to forgive this blasphemer who cared not what he did."[36] That he was not naïve about human character—that Europeans were not by their nature any more humane

35. Wesley, *Letters*, viii., 265.
36. Equiano, *Narrative*, 177.

than the people in the Americas—is evident in a remark he made close to the end of his life: "keep me from all such Rascals as I have met with in London."[37]

On two occasions he tried to return to Africa. In 1779 he applied to the Bishop of London for ordination, so that he could be a missionary to Africa, but was turned down. Subsequently, he was appointed as Commissary for Stores for a 1787 expedition to resettle former slaves in Sierra Leone, but experienced one final act of betrayal when he was fired, having made public a pattern of mismanagement on the part of the other leaders. His work for Africa was not to be in Africa but in Britain, giving voice, respect and dignity to black seamen and other poor African men and women who daily negotiated for their very survival in the colonies and in London. By now a Methodist, he traveled throughout the British Isles, promoting his famous book, lecturing powerfully against the slave trade, and networking with his allies. What was perhaps most remarkable about his efforts was that in an age of increasing political discord and denominational competition, he was supported by people from all over the political spectrum and from every denomination.

In our age it is too easy to underestimate his accomplishments. Abolitionism was a stand against the era's common sense and perceived economic interest, while slavery was supported by the press, parliament, and the intelligentsia. The botanist Carl Linnaeus, who founded the system for classifying the natural world still in use today, placed Africans in a category he labeled *homo monstrous*. John Locke thought owning people not at all distinct from holding other forms of property, a view shared by Thomas Jefferson. The most powerful eighteenth-century Enlightenment thinker in Britain, David Hume, wrote that "I am apt to suspect the Negroes to be naturally inferior to the Whites. . . . No ingenious manufactures amongst them, no arts, no sciences."[38] In her review of the *Interesting Narrative* Mary Wollstonecraft, the leading feminist in the late eighteenth century was dismissive of the importance of Equiano's conversion to his achievements, commenting that "The long account of his religious sentiments and conversion to Methodism, is rather tiresome."[39] By living by his pen, Equiano demolished the argument that Africans were an inferior people, as his pen had condemned the argument that Africans were less human than

37. Walvin, *An African's Life*, 165.

38. Hume, *Essays*, i., 252, n. 1.

39. Carretta, *Equiano*, 332.

Europeans. Only much later would scientific research catch up to Equiano's faith-filled thinking.

An Igbo proverb holds that "No one can wrestle with his *chi*."[40] And yet, is that not precisely what Olaudah Equiano had done, and not just on the day he became a Christian? Readers of the *Interesting Narrative* witnessed a man who, in spite of enslavement and attendant humiliations, went from illiterate African animist to sophisticated European Christian, which surely raised for them the issue defenders of the slave trade endeavored to cover up: Africans were no less humans made in the image of God than were Europeans. His story destroyed control of the moral narrative regarding the slave trade and slavery itself, deceptively spun by its defenders as merely about economics and national self interest. Equiano's Christian identity led him back to his origins, hence his self-description "the African" on the title page of his *Interesting Narrative*. At the same time that identity led him forwards, from his all-consuming desire as a slave to earn his freedom to a passion to free enslaved Africans and champion the rights of fellow Afro-Britons. Not only were the two not in conflict, they mutually supported each other. Sometimes speaking from a British and on other occasions an African perspective, he was "a citizen of the world,"[41] perhaps history's first global citizen.

His text

I then, in the greatest agony, requested the divine Creator, that he would grant me a small space of time to repent of my follies and vile iniquities, which I felt was grievous. The Lord, in his manifold mercies, was pleased to grant my request, and being yet in a state of time, the sense of God's mercies were so great on my mind when I awoke, that my strength entirely failed me for many minutes, and I was exceedingly weak. This was the first spiritual mercy I ever was sensible of, and being on praying ground, as soon as I recovered a little strength, and got out of bed and dressed myself I invoked heaven, from my inmost soul, and fervently begged that God would never again permit me to blaspheme his most holy name. The Lord, who is long-suffering and full of compassion to such poor rebels as we are, condescended to hear and answer. I felt that I was altogether unholy, and saw clearly what a bad use I had made of the faculties I was endowed with: they

40. Edwards and Shaw, "Invisible *Chi*," 149.

41. Potkay, "Equiano and Spiritual Autobiography," 679.

were given me to glorify God with; I thought, therefore, I had better want them here, and enter into life eternal, than abuse them and be cast into hell fire. I prayed to be directed, if there were any holier persons than those with whom I was acquainted, that the Lord would point them out to me. I appealed to the searcher of hearts, whether I did not wish to love him more, and serve him better. Notwithstanding all this, the reader may easily discern, if a believer, that I was still in nature's darkness. At length I hated the house in which I lodged, because God's most holy name was blasphemed in it; then I saw the word of God verified, viz., "Before they call, I will answer; and while they are yet speaking I will hear" (Isaiah 65:24).

The Interesting Narrative of the Life of Olaudah Equiano or Gustavus Vassa, the African. Written by Himself (1789)

Questions

1. Ponder the full title of our subject's autobiography: *The Interesting Narrative of the Life of Olaudah Equiano or Gustavus Vassa, the African. Written by Himself.* What meaning might that title have?

2. Was Equiano *lucky*?

3. What did Equiano use to define who he was, in contrast to his circumstances or experiences?

4. How was the trajectory of history different because Equiano became a believer?

5. If you have ever experienced prejudice, what was helpful in reading this chapter? If you have not experienced prejudice, how might Equiano's life nevertheless inspire you?

For further reading

Carretta, Vincent. *Equiano, the African: Biography of a Self-Made Man.* New York: Penguin, 2006.

Equiano, Olaudah. *The Interesting Narrative of the Life of Olaudah Equiano.* New York: Modern Library, 2004; http://books.google.com/books.

Walvin, James. *An African's Life: The Life and Times of Olaudah Equiano, 1745–1797.* London: Cassell, 1998.

Chapter 3

Hannah More

Story: Redeeming culture and society

> Philanthropy is rather justice than charity . . .
> to assist their own laboring poor is a kind of natural debt,
> which persons who possess great landed property owe to those
> from the sweat of whose brow they derive their comforts, and even
> their riches.
> Hannah More, aged 53

HANNAH MORE WAS THE most successful female author and arguably the most influential woman of her era. Selina Hastings anticipated her attempts to reform society; More was one of the original subscribers to Olaudah Equiano's *Interesting Narrative*; and she was a close friend of William Wilberforce, the subject of the next chapter. "Who has heard of her now?" asks More's latest biographer.[1] The answer should be, all who wish to contemplate the application of courage to the quest for a more just society.

Hannah More was born in 1745 outside of Bristol, the fourth of five daughters of a farmer's daughter and a not very well off schoolmaster who saw that his children were well-educated, training them to be teachers. Having been "born with more desires than guineas"[2] as they recalled

---

1. Stott, *Hannah More*, p. vii.
2. More, *Poetical Works*, p. ix.

their shabby-genteel circumstances, early on in their lives the sisters ben-efitted from encouragement: Hannah remembered a clergyman next-door neighbor, who "first awakened me to some sense of serious things."[3] While still teenagers, the three oldest More daughters established a school for girls in Bristol, soon to be famous for combining piety and intellect. The precocious Hannah completed her education there, and then in her mid-teens began teaching at the school. While lacking formal training, she was a natural teacher, throughout her life exhibiting a love of children. At age sixteen she wrote her first play, to be performed by her students, which was later published and widely read. More herself was closely involved with the Theatre Royal Bristol, which staged another play of hers. It would seem, then, that from her youth More's vocation was to be a writer. But to what end? Fame, she was to discover, can be fatal.

At twenty-two Hannah More became engaged to William Turner, a wealthy middle-aged landowner. However, what began as a good match turned into every woman's nightmare. The engagement lasted for six years but Turner could not bring himself to realize the wedding, on three sepa-rate occasions postponing the date for the nuptials. Having lost patience with her irresolute fiancé, in 1773 More finally broke off the engagement. The first of many moments of adversity in her life, the affair was person-ally humiliating and produced some sort of nervous breakdown. But in compensation for having given up her share of the school in preparation for the marriage, Turner paid her an annuity of £200, giving More the financial independence to become a woman of letters.

Having overcome this episode, in her late twenties Hannah More and some of her sisters began spending each winter season in London. As a result of her lively mind and engaging personality, More was able to net-work with the artistic, literary, and political giants of her age—the artist Sir Joshua Reynolds, the actor-theatre manager David Garrick, the writers Samuel Johnson and Horace Walpole, and the politician Edmund Burke (for whom she worked when he campaigned in Bristol for election to Par-liament). When not electioneering she wrote, beginning with social com-mentary. Her published poetry went into several editions. Garrick directed her play *Percy*, a drama set in medieval England and staged in 1777 at the Theatre Royal Covent Garden, the top playhouse in the country. *Percy* was an enormous success—both in promoting her fame and in earning her a great deal of money.

3. Roberts, *Memoirs*, ii., 106.

More was stage struck: In less than a decade by exploiting her talent she had become one of the central figures in London society. Only thirty-two, she was praised for her poetry, her plays and other writing, and her conversation. Samuel Johnson termed her "the most powerful versificatrix in the English language."[4] More was a key figure in the famous Bluestockings, a circle of well-connected, predominantly upper-class London women, which gave her an entry into the world of the British aristocracy. For a provincial female of very modest social background she had spectacularly made it to the very center of British culture and society—an incongruity those jealous of her success were not hesitant to point out.

There was, however, a certain insecurity in her mind, or perhaps it was a sense of the emptiness of fame—"the applause of the world"[5] as she once put it. Looking backward at these years, More believed she made too many compromises—in dress, behavior, and literary style. Everything she wrote was a best-seller, and success turned her head, providing the complete fulfillment of her deep desire for attention. More had always been religious—indeed, she was by now a strict observer of the Sabbath—but she had never experienced a deep personal faith. Being merely religious allowed her to justify her social activities, publications, and reputation as means for providing a positive influence on a morally corrupt high society. Reading a 1790 book of More's, "good person" rather than God's person might have been how she would have described herself. By this later time she understood charity not popularity was "the most lovely offspring of religion,"[6] and as a mark of the believer. She came to understand that the Christian faith was not a performance but, in her words, "a turning of the whole mind to God."[7] Thus good works and moral living demonstrated faith but could never be mere substitutes for it.

When her friend Garrick died in 1779 More lost her enthusiasm for the theatre and the London social scene generally, and ceased writing for the stage. Her last play had been panned by critics, while another playwright publicly accused More of stealing her concept. Perhaps More realized that the theatre was not the best venue for putting forward her ideas. She wrote at the time: "I find my dislike of what are called public diversions greater than ever . . . I could be very well content . . . to live in London, without ever

4. Boswell, *Johnson*, iii., 294, n. 5.
5. More, *Works*, iii., 421.
6. Ibid., i., 260.
7. More, *Estimate of Religion*, 60.

again setting foot in a public place."[8] These words suggest a second moment of crisis in her life, less than a decade after the broken engagement—revealing despondency regarding her life's purpose.

More became the companion of Garrick's widow for the next twenty London winter seasons, remained part of the Bluestocking circle, and corresponded with a host of important people. Her poem, "The Bas Bleu; or Conversation," published in 1787, was a witty celebration of her friendships and the intellectual culture they represented, and more profoundly that "conversation/Emerges into reformation."[9] Negatively, it's fair to say More still struggled between wanting literary and social fame and wanting goodness, desiring notice and attention but longing to use her position to do good alongside doing well.

By the 1780s More had become *the* person to pay attention to. For such people, who are always listened to, the danger lies in not listening to others—particularly society's have-nots. But fame did not protect her from her times: this was an era of character assassination, and she endured her share of public attacks. Assailed for her strict sabbatarianism as "holy Hannah" and derided as a "Bishop in petticoats,"[10] she was as well put down for her obscure provincial background. She was harshly criticized for engaging in over-flattery to gain attention and at the same time condemned for being less critical of books and persons than she ought. One of her critics, speaking about her, stated: "Don't you hate a person who thinks ill of nobody?"[11]

It was at this moment, 1780, that her friend Frances Reynolds, sister of the famous artist and an accomplished painter in her own right, created her portrait of More. The artist's subject, aged thirty-five, poses as a literary celebrity. About to apply pen to paper, what is it she is contemplating on the eve of her conversion? Knowing what

Hannah More
By Edward Scriven, after Frances Reynolds
© National Portrait Gallery, London

8. Roberts, *Memoirs*, i., 57.

9. More, *Works*, i., 15.

10. Walpole, *Private Correspondence*, iv., 525; *Cobbett's Political Register*, April 20, 1822.

11. D'Arbley, *Diary and Letters*, 169.

we know from her later life, is it that fame is elusive and vanity never satis-fying? Is it that though her instincts were conventional regarding women's place in the world, with some irony she had embarked on a very public and active calling? Was it the text, that God chooses the weak things of the world to shame the strong (1 Cor 1:27)?

Conversion

In a letter to her sisters written the same year as the portrait, More stated she and Mrs. Garrick might have passed for Oxford or Cambridge pro-fessors, for they "read as much as any two doctors of either University."[12] Her taste in reading was wide-ranging: she consumed works by and about Puritans, but also read skeptics such as Hume, Voltaire, and Rousseau. A friend sent her a book by the Reverend John Newton, of the hymn *Amazing Grace* fame, and More began attending his church in London. Although by reputation Newton was a poor speaker, she found herself attracted to the story of his salvation, from a life "so big with mischief"[13] to becoming an Anglican priest.

Newton's appeal for orthodox beliefs and for Christians to go out and change the world applied one of the core teachings of Jesus. When asked what he considered the greatest commandments to be, Jesus encour-aged his contemporaries that after they had learned to love God that they were to work out that love in their relationships with those human beings around them. For Newton this had come to mean ending the slave trade, telling More that "whatever politicians may think, I assuredly know there is a righteous Judge who governs the earth. He calls upon us to redress the injured."[14] So, Newton advised More (and William Wilberforce): you have great gifts; now believe in the giver of the gifts and do the work of that righteous judge in the public sphere.

Pious and regular in her Sunday church attendance and committed to reading serious literature, More discovered that while such eccentrici-ties were tolerated in provincial Bristol she was ridiculed in swinging Lon-don, which caused her to reflect on why she did what she did, and in turn helped lead her to become a believer. So did her growing sense—evident in the letters passing between More and Newton—that God desired "vital

12. Roberts, *Memoirs*, i., 167.

13. Stott, *Hannah More*, 82.

14. Roberts, *Memoirs*, i., 384.

religion,"[15] that a personal relationship was much lovelier than behavior aimed at earning merit. It remains unknown whether her Christian conversion was a sudden event or a gradual change in mind and heart. When she told Newton "the reform never begins,"[16] he encouraged her that the very awareness of failure was a mile marker on the road to conversion. It seems reasonable to assume that, like Saul, one moment she was religious and the next a new creation, that she turned from the notion that she could please God by doing good to faith in Jesus as her Lord and savior. As she later put it, "Christianity is not a religion of forms and modes and decencies: it is being transformed into the image of God."[17]

Whatever it was that happened, it permanently and completely changed her life. As evidence, she turned to more distinctly Christian writing and work. Newton became her spiritual director, and she came to draw upon him, the Bishop of London, and a growing network of evangelicals such as William Wilberforce, for friendship, spiritual encouragement, and accountability. She was particularly impressed with Wilberforce, fourteen years her junior: "That young gentleman's character is one of the most extraordinary I ever knew for talents, virtue, and piety. It is difficult not to grow wiser and better every time one converses with him."[18] And yet she found excellence outside her circle of evangelical Anglicans, including many who were not believers. Writing to a friend in 1783, More noted that, "Very transcendent genius in any book or persons excites in me pleasures even to rapture."[19] This should be a mark of the believer—to prize merit wherever it exists.

The Clapham evangelicals, introduced in detail in the next chapter, were for her an alternative network More developed during the several years following her conversion. In her existing circles "polite" usually trumped "right," with a consequential indifference to individual and societal corruption. The Clapham community was serious about its personal walk with God and anticipated a claim often attributed to William Temple, a twentieth-century Archbishop of Canterbury: "The Church is the only institution that exists for the benefit of those who are not its members." At the same time More stayed intellectually attached to society—Charles

15. Stott, *Hannah More*, p. x.

16. Roberts, *Memoirs*, i., 387.

17. More, *Works*, i., 436.

18. Wilberforce and Wilberforce, *Life*, i., 72.

19. Jones, *Hannah More*, 45.

Wesley had advised her to remain in the fashionable world to retain her impact on the rich and powerful. But she gradually redeemed her time, detaching herself from those things that, in the words of one early biographer, "however agreeable to her taste and talents, kept her from answering the higher vocation."[20] This is old-fashioned language that makes an important point. In her journal she wrote self-critically about problems she shared with all believers, that "my mind rambles through a thousand vain, trifling, and worldly thoughts, . . . but seldom sticks close to God."[21] Spending more and more of her time reading the Bible and theology, as God reached out to her, she fell in love with Christ—with all of her heart, mind, soul, and strength—and in so doing came to love her neighbor as herself.

Calling

More's conversion revealed to her how much she loved the world. In her words, "I had rather *work* for God than *meditate* on him."[22] And so she began writing with a purpose other than attention or profit. More published *Sacred Dramas* in 1782, Bible stories rewritten in the form of dialogues. Critics panned the work, and her publisher commented that More was now "too good a Christian for an author,"[23] but strong sales suggested it had found a receptive audience. She also wrote what were then called conduct books, what would today be social criticism. These included *Thoughts on the Importance of the Manners of the Great to General Society* (1788), which maintained that the elite was ultimately responsible for the conduct of those who observed them—the one thing those at the top did not want to hear. Thus, "To expect to reform the poor while the opulent are corrupt, is to throw odors into the stream while the springs are poisoned."[24] As one of those very people, More was aware she "did not live up to my song."[25]

One conversation More had is revealing, with an unnamed but beautiful and accomplished woman of fashion, "surrounded by flatterers, and sunk in dissipation."[26] More asked her if she was happy.

20. Roberts, *Memoirs*, i., 132.

21. Ibid., i., 551.

22. Ibid., i., 260.

23. More, *Poetical Works*, p. xii.

24. More, *Works*, v., 204.

25. Roberts, *Memoirs*, i., 416.

26. Ibid., i., 342.

> Happy! she said, no; she was miserable; she despised the society
> she lived in, and had no enjoyment of the pleasures in which her
> life was consumed; but what could she do? She could not be singu-
> lar—she must do as her acquaintance did.[27]

Because rank had it privileges, it took a great deal of courage to publish *Thoughts on the Importance of the Manners of the Great to General Society*. In fact, More found an avid readership among the very people she feared would shun her. That the book became a best-seller suggests a substantial public existed, one waiting for someone with the courage to say the things More did.

Her next publication was *An Estimate of the Religion of the Fashionable World* (1790), which argued that Christians were negligent because they had disengaged moral behavior from belief—the one thing nominal Christians did not want to hear. Raising an alarm that "practical irreligion"[28] was far more of a national threat than unbelief, her challenge to contemporaries was to replace unrestrained consumerism with a "desire to please *Him*."[29] In response to *Religion of the Fashionable World*, More was burned in effigy by students at a prestigious private school. Following Christ by fulfilling our calling will likely provoke some negative responses, and the believer should be prepared for such reactions. In between *Manners of the Great* and *Religion of the Fashionable World*, More opened her first Sunday school for the poor. So over the course of a decade Hannah More explored what she was supposed to do for the rest of her life, shedding the London world—as an end—and seeking to redeem her culture and society.

Achievements

Most of us are frustrated with our society or government at least some of the time, and dream that a fundamental change can make things right. Historically, the dream has all too often morphed into a nightmare. Ponder the effects on actual people of four twentieth-century events—the Bolshevik revolution of 1917, the Nazi seizure of power (1933), the Chinese revolution of 1949, or the Khmer Rouge insurrection in Cambodia (1975). These

27. Ibid., i., 342–43.
28. More, *Works*, i., 277.
29. More, *Estimate of Religion*, 58.

four *actual* revolutions and their aftermath resulted in the deaths of well over 100 million people. Yet each began with the goal of human perfection.

In troubled times social turmoil followed by a critical mass of personal choices is capable of producing revolution. It can be argued that no one played a more important role in preventing revolution in late eighteenth- and early nineteenth-century Britain than did Hannah More—not the prime minister William Pitt, not Lord Nelson and the British navy, not Edmund Burke and his book *Reflections on the Revolution in France,* not the police nor the army, but one physically frail woman—Hannah More. Nearly fifty, she now made the move from social to political commentator, in response to one of the most tumultuous moments of her country's history.

In 1793 More published *Village Politics,* a popular tract designed to confront head on the arguments of Thomas Paine's 1791 *The Rights of Man.* Paine's simple rhetoric and its inexpensive price made his book a huge popular success. In *Rights of Man* Paine argued that "If universal peace, civilization and commerce are ever to be the happy lot of man, it cannot be accomplished but by a revolution in the systems of government."[30] To his way of thinking each generation had the right to rewrite constitutional arrangements in their own interest. He proposed the use of power to redistribute national wealth, in Britain and globally. Powerful ideas—and powerfully tempting. No writer more effectively countered *Rights of Man* than did Hannah More in *Village Politics,* which treated the implications of political theory not in the abstract but by creating a real world with which readers could identify.

Knowing common people far better than Paine—because they were a part of her life—More proposed that there was a spiritual basis for society that molded both persons and national institutions. Only with great peril should they be remolded. (More may have been thinking as much about the French philosopher Rousseau as Paine. Rousseau's writings promoted promiscuity by women as liberating. More responded in *Strictures* that such an argument "gives vice so natural an air of virtue . . . elevating a crime into a principle."[31]) Good order produced freedom and true respect for the less well-off. In *Village Politics* common sense is contrasted with the implied consequences of enthusiasm for revolution not backed by understanding of what might happen if the world were indeed to be turned upside down.

30. Paine, *Works,* 184.
31. More, *Works,* i., 318.

Here's a brief excerpt from *Village Politics*. The draw is both word play and the political philosophy. It's good to read it out loud because most people affected by it would have heard it read. (Do your best to mimic the accents of eighteenth-century British laborers.)

A dialogue between Jack Anvil, the blacksmith, and Tom Hod, the mason.

Jack: What's the matter, Tom? Why dost look so dismal?

Tom: Dismal, indeed! Well enough I may.

Jack: What! is the old mare dead? or work scarce?

Tom: No, no, work's plenty enough, if a man had but the heart to go to it.

Jack: What book art reading? Why dost look so like a hang-dog?

Tom: (Looking on his book) Cause enough. I find here that I am very unhappy, and very miserable; which I should never have known, if I had not had the good luck to meet with this book. Oh, 'tis a precious book!

Jack: A good sign tho'—that you can't find out you're unhappy, without looking into a book for it! What is the matter?

Tom: Matter? Why I want liberty.

Jack: Liberty? That's bad, indeed! What! has anyone fetched a warrant for thee? Come, man, cheer up, I'll be bound for thee. Thou art an honest fellow in the main, tho' thou doest tipple and prate a little too much at the Rose and Crown.

Tom: No, no, I want a new constitution.

Jack: Indeed! Why, I thought thou hadst been a desperately healthy fellow. Send for the doctor directly.

Tom: I'm not sick; I want liberty and equality, and the rights of man.

Jack: Oh, now I understand thee. What! thou art a leveller and a republican, I warrant!

Tom: I'm a friend to the people. I want a reform.

Jack: Then the shortest way is to mend thyself.

Tom: But I want a *general* reform.

Jack: Then let everyone mend one.

Village Politics ends with Tom accepting Jack's reasoning and its consequences:

Jack: While Old England is safe, I'll glory in her, and pray for her; and when she is in danger, I'll fight for her, and die for her.[32]

32. Ibid., i., 58, 62.

There's a universal application here, as More knew full well, deriving from nearly every page of the Bible: the problem is not some abstraction, *society*, it's us—you and me. If I'm truly serious about fixing society, rather than just talking about it, I need to begin with myself. The bad news is that as many times as I tried, working alone I could never fix myself. The good news, the gospel, points us to how we might get fixed, and More pointed there as well. She was later to write in her diary, "Christianity is a broad basis. *Bible* Christianity is what I love; . . . a Christianity practical and pure, which teaches holiness, humility, repentance, and faith in Christ; and which after summing up all the evangelical graces, declares that the greatest of these is charity."[33] Love or revolution?

More followed up *Village Politics* with a pamphlet attacking the statements of a French politician whose atheistic rhetoric helped unleash attacks on French Catholic priests, driving many into exile. Those who came to Britain were welcomed by More, who dedicated the profits of her pamphlet to their support. Because she praised the character and courage of French priests she was now accused of being pro-Catholic (in troubled times it is often true that no good deed goes unpunished). In her age and ours political upheavals unleash incoherent opinions. Nevertheless, looking backward, it is hard to underestimate More's role in saving her country from revolution.

If the first arena of her heart and mind at work was about thinking globally—what made her country and its culture worth preserving—the second saw her acting locally. The historical context of what follows is a society with serious shortcomings: having no provision for public education, Britain was a nation of citizens who couldn't read.

In 1789, encouraged by Wilberforce, Hannah More and her younger sister Martha founded a school for the poor at Cheddar, in Somersetshire, a village of extreme poverty that had been without a resident clergyman for forty years. The sisters had visited "every house in the place,"[34] seeing in the homes of the poor "more misery in a week than some people believe exists in the whole world."[35] Having studied the problem of poverty first-hand, within a decade the More sisters were supporting and administering sixteen Sunday schools in neighboring towns, teaching thousands of poor boys and girls to read (and encouraging them to read to their illiter-

---

33. Roberts, *Memoirs*, ii., 111.

34. Ibid., i., 389.

35. Chatterton, *Memorials of Admiral Gambier*, 291.

ate parents), helping them learn to do what was right by applying biblical principles to everyday activities, and teaching them skills that would help them later in life—in sum, promoting human dignity. Believing firmly that Christian teaching should be the basis of all education, Hannah More wrote many of the books used in the schools.

These were not the Sunday schools of modern memory. Instruction occurred on Sunday because that was the one day of the week the majority of poor people didn't work. In the establishment of the More sisters there was in addition a Sunday evening service for parents. On Tuesday nights teachers read a chapter of the Bible and explained difficult words. Wednesday evenings saw adult classes. Girls were taught household techniques as well as useful skills so they could be employed. There were job outplacement services. The schools were centers of social life in their villages.

The More sisters kept the schools afloat by their constant attention, traveling the countryside on horseback every Sunday from May to December no matter what the weather because, in Hannah's words, "The simple idea of being cared for has always appeared to me to be a very cheering one."[36] More continued this work for three decades until in her mid-seventies ill health forced her to stop. As a measure of their usefulness, three of the schools survived into the twentieth century, and they serve as something of a model for what would today be called continuing education and lifelong learning.

In More's time the schools were extensively criticized. Radicals complained about the use of the Bible as the basic text for instruction and other Christian content. Nominal Christians and others in the religious establishment feared the schools were promoting Methodism, and though More remained a faithful Anglican they illogically accused her of being a Methodist. One clergyman used his pulpit to preach against the local More school. The wife of another clergyman protested that at a Monday night prayer meeting men actually gave personal testimonies about their spiritual state. Another complaint was that "a vast number of those brought up at Sunday school were wandering from their proper callings, had become fanatical preachers, had deemed themselves qualified to hold disputations, had turned skeptic and infidel and anarchist."[37] One wealthy local farmer asked More, "if property is not to rule what is to become of us?"[38] With

36. Roberts, *Memoirs*, i., 503.

37. *Anti-Jacobin* 7 (1800), 216.

38. Jones, *Hannah More*, 169.

so much criticism from all over political and social spectrums, the More sisters must have been doing something right. But notice also they were laypersons; sensing their own church had failed its duties toward the poor, they did not hesitate to take initiatives, even in the face of widespread criticism.

Engaging culture led More to thinking, which in turn led her to writing and then to activism. Like coming to Christ, she wrote her way to engaging in works of social justice and cultural projects. Thus More published *Slavery, A Poem* (1788) in support of the first parliamentary debate aimed at abolishing the slave trade, helping contribute to a turning point in public opinion. She used her reputation and gifts to do a good work, which God had prepared in advance for her to do, knowing it would be unpopular among many of her readers. Her native Bristol's wealth was based in large part on the slave trade and slave-produced sugar; some parents of the pupils in the More sisters' school were respectable merchants connected to the slave trade. Yet in her mind morality trumped economics: the heart of the issue was that slavery was incompatible with Christianity, because both black and white were children of God.

More used strong images in the poem—of a slave raid that led to an African village being set on fire, of families being torn apart, "Horrors of deepest, deadliest guilt."[39] She in effect apologized to Africans for what her countrymen had done: "They are *not* Christians who infest thy shore,"[40] but willful white savages. And she praised Quakers who had freed their slaves: "*their* doctrines rule their lives."[41] Africans, like Britons, were created in the image of God: "They still are men, and men shou'd still be free."[42]

> Shall Britain, where the soul of freedom reigns,
> Forge chains for others she herself disdains?
> Forbid it, Heaven! O let the nations know
> The liberty she loves she will bestow.[43]

As well as her writing, More promoted a boycott of slave-grown sugar. Her courage is all the more remarkable in that she was the first female involved in the organized opposition to the slave trade, and her perseverance is also

39. More, *Works,* i., 28.
40. Ibid., i., 29.
41. Ibid.
42. Ibid., i., 28.
43. Ibid., i., 29.

remarkable: she helped lead the organization that fought the battle for the twenty years it took to triumph. With others she followed the biblical mandate to remember those who were being mistreated as if they themselves were suffering, and in so doing encouraged other white Britons to reject the current "proud philosophy"[44] that applied Enlightenment thought to support racial inequality:

[Africans] have heads to think, and hearts to feel,
And souls to act, with firm, tho' erring, zeal;
For they have keen affections, kind desires,
Love strong as death, and active patriot fires.[45]

Several years later More began a new venture. In the Cheap Repository tracts More brought together two of her concerns—politics and the poor—as well as her experience as a popular writer. The tracts were a series of vividly written moral tales and ballads as well as sermons, prayers, and Bible readings. Published between 1795 and 1798, the tracts provided a working and middle class readership an alternative to the degrading cheap literature supplied by the mainstream publishing market, which promoted superstitions such as fortune-telling and celebrated drunkenness and rioting. More read the worst of these works, studied the technique, and then used the form to transform. (Imagine today forcing yourself to watch a steady diet of television reality shows, listen to vitriolic talk radio, surf the Internet, and read what's in the stands at the checkout in your grocery store.) But rather than merely criticizing popular literature she emulated it: "It has occurred to me to write a variety of things, somewhere between vicious papers and hymns, for it is vain to write what people will not read."[46] Because, as the Bishop of London believed, More understood both "the cottage and the palace,"[47] her test was whether she could offer a viable alternative to what she was condemning. She chose to build up, not just tear down.

Her formula was to use a strong narrative to tell the life of an individual, almost always poor, who faced a difficult challenge, leading either to transformation (self-mastery, a strengthened marriage or parent-child relationship, mutual dependence of rich and poor, faith) or degradation and death. The works had woodcuts for visual interest and catchy titles, like *The*

44. Ibid., i., 27.
45. Ibid.
46. Jones, *Hannah More*, 139.
47. More, *Works*, i., 28.

History of Idle Jack Brown: Containing the Merry Story of the Mountebank, with some Account of the Bay Mare Smiler—who wouldn't want to read that! The great strengths of More's publications were that they were drawn from life, designed to introduce real human beings with all their vices and virtues, and that in terms of price hit their intended audience. The tracts found their way into homes of the poor throughout the British Isles, as well as prisons, hospitals, and the armed forces. Her marketing approach was brilliant, having the tracts sold by peddlers on the streets who, More wrote a friend, "have no objection to goodness, if it were but profitable."[48] By the end of the first year of publication 2,000,000 had been distributed—twenty times Paine's *Rights of Man*.

In one tract More wrote, *The History of Mr. Fantom, the new-fashioned Philosopher and Reformist,* a worker expresses contempt for those who engage in speculative abstractions rather than participating in the lives of the poor:

> To love mankind so dearly, and yet avoid all opportunities of doing good; to have such a noble zeal for the millions, and to feel so little compassion for the units; surely none but a philosopher could indulge so much philanthropy.[49]

Equally worthy of mockery was that "in his zeal to make the whole world free and happy, [Fantom] was too prudent to include his wife."[50] This is in contrast to the efforts of Mrs. Fantom and her daughter, who engage in charitable efforts to address poverty in their neighborhood, and the thoughts of a poor man in another tract, *The Shepherd of Salisbury Plain*, who cannot stand seeing shoeless and sockless children first and foremost as a matter of human dignity.

Rather than philosophers and political propagandists the profoundest insights come from the least pretentious, like that shepherd or in another tract Farmer Worthy: "If Jesus Christ died for no one particular rank, class, or community, then there is no one rank, class, or community exempt from his laws."[51] Rather than lecturing the poor not to look for justice until they reached heaven, More's writings held out the goal of a Christian society which, based on godly, face-to-face relationships between rich and poor

48. Roberts, *Memoirs*, 473.
49. More, *Works*, i., 124.
50. Ibid., i., 123.
51. Ibid., i., 145.

would be far more integrated than the Britain of her times. The ideal is expressed by a down-to-earth female character who explains to the local clergyman the positive change that had overtaken the wealthy in her vicinity. An economic downturn had "led them to get more acquainted with the local wants of their poorer brethren, and to interest themselves in their comfort."[52] Hard times had in fact "brought the affluent to a nearer knowledge of the persons and characters of their indigent neighbors; it has literally brought rich and poor to meet together."[53]

More personally penned 50 of the 114 tracts as well as organizing the project and securing underwriting, drawing on her sisters and the Clapham network to write the others. This was a huge strain for a woman in her fifties who was also running over a dozen Sunday schools. But as a number of the tracts were written specifically for poor women to help them understand they might play an important social role, while others confronted the slave trade at a time the Abolition Committee was experiencing defeat in its propaganda campaign, it is important to notice how her projects aimed at redeeming culture complemented each other.

Once again deeds followed words. More complained to magistrates when bakers sold the poor underweight and contaminated loaves of bread; she taught villagers how to run community projects, such as village ovens; she addressed the physical and spiritual needs of the elderly in almshouses; she lectured those in the higher classes about their duty to assist the poor— including lobbying one of Prime Minister Pitt's advisers. Along with several friends, during the winter of 1817 when in midst of a depression 300 zinc miners were laid off, she provided for their families and purchased all the ore they produced. Regarding the Sunday schools she had clergymen, farmers, and gentry wait on the poor at annual feasts. In the tracts and related works she let the poor know the well-to-do had faults and the great understand that those beneath them socially had virtues.

Perhaps the most enigmatic element of Hannah More's life work concerns her writing about women's roles, because in many ways she was quite conventional and a social and political conservative. But she had lived as an independent woman since her late twenties. And as far back as the 1770s she had written, "The women of this country . . . are of a religion . . . which does not condemn its followers to indolent seclusion from the world, but assigns them the dangerous though more honourable province, of living

52. Ibid., i., 172.
53. Ibid.

uncorrupted by it."[54] In some ways More's writing reflected an assumption that women were morally superior to men. The huge audience among women for her writings suggests she tapped a market for many like herself, who found "seen and not heard" an inadequate model for life because they longed to learn and practice active virtue.

More produced a series of conduct books, the most famous being *Strictures on the Modern System of Female Education* (1799). *Strictures* urged that education for women be founded on Christian teaching for living the moral life, so that discussion should be the standard pedagogy rather than learning by rote. The message of *Strictures* was that women had been short-changed, fobbed off with a trivial education that left them unfitted to be companionable wives, rational mothers, or moral examples to the wider society. More proposed that women read works of logic and difficult texts such as John Locke's *Essay on Human Understanding*. She thought that "serious study serves to harden the mind for more trying conflicts."[55] The notion that education should be preparation for life was very advanced for the time, and in some ways *Strictures* can be considered a feminist tract. In More's mind, because "piety maintains no natural war with elegance," *Strictures* was also a book for believers, because life is "a school to fit us for eternity."[56]

Her call to women was not to an unreflective submission or withdrawal from the world but "as patriots at once firm and feminine."[57] She argued that females should use modesty and humility to engage in the most important public work imaginable, the regeneration of society. The woman's *profession*, in the word's older sense, was to play a central role in alleviating poverty and reforming their communities, less through money than by education and life choices.

> Young ladies should be accustomed to set apart a fixed part of their time, as sacred to the poor, whether in relieving, instructing, or working for them; and the performance of this duty must not be left to the event of contingent circumstances, or the operation of accidental impressions; but it must be established into a principle, and wrought into a habit. A specific portion of the day must be

54. Ibid., ii, 554.
55. Ibid., i., 344.
56. Ibid., i., 326, 323.
57. Ibid., i., 313.

allotted to it, on which no common engagement must be allowed to intrench.[58]

One of her fictional characters is Mrs. Jones, a newly impoverished widow with no money but much wisdom gained from extensive reading of books on economics. She motivates her equally poor neighbors not to imitate the elite by consuming white bread and tea but encouraging them to bake their own brown bread and brew their own beer—which would have the salutatory effect of keeping their husbands away from pubs. More's argument for her fellow females was, change the home and you will change the world. The implications of this for us grow clearer with each passing year: The poor and women have always suffered the most from the demise of the strong family. If any single person invented the model for the modern public woman it was Hannah More. And once again because of what she wrote More was vilified by many in the political and religious establishments.

Her most ambitious conduct book, *Hints towards Forming the Character of a Young Princess* (1805) was published anonymously for the nine-year-old Princess Charlotte Augusta (daughter of the Prince of Wales and thus after her father heir to the throne). In suggesting a regimen of reading for the princess, More made the argument that education, even for royalty, was in the end about character formation—which made study of the nation's past the centerpiece: "History is the glass by which the royal mind is dressed."[59] As in the future she was to be a model for her people, Charlotte should look backward to exemplary rulers of Britain—especially female royals. As a child the princess wrote that her tutor read to her from *Hints* "an hour or two every day," lamenting that "I *am not quite good enough* for that yet,"[60] although on her eighteenth birthday she elected to reread More's book.

Although long a critic of contemporary fiction because of the genre's frivolity and its promotion of vice and infidelity, More chose to write a novel. *Coelebs in Search of a Wife* (1808) turned out to be a best-seller, an essay on finding a moral partner masquerading as a courtship novel. The text offered women authority in British society, urging them to take the lead in defining their own sphere: "Charity is the calling of a lady; the care of the poor is her profession."[61] More reinforced the argument of *Strictures*

58. Ibid., i., 332.
59. Ibid., ii., 16.
60. Aspinall, *Letters of Princess Charlotte*, 38.
61. More, *Coelebs*, 226.

on the Modern System of Female Education that women should aspire to be useful rather than ornamental. The magnitude of a companionate marriage was clear: "The prime comfort in a companion for life is the delightful hope that she will be a companion for eternity."[62]

More's writing was once again matched by activism: she initiated and endowed a series of female benefit clubs, encouraging women to become self-reliant by saving money for future emergency occasions—sickness, pregnancy, and for their funerals. Prior to More's activities, such cooperative ventures existed only for men. More's clubs, two of which survived well into the twentieth century, had hundreds of members. One obituary claimed that, "What Wilberforce was among men, Hannah More was among women."[63]

At fifty-three Hannah More confessed her weaknesses in a 1789 diary entry, including her temper, speaking rashly or harshly, worldly imaginations, and over-anxiety. She also experienced serious health issues, suffering from migraine headaches, chronic asthma, bronchitis, stomach problems, fevers, other maladies, and occasional psychological collapse. Her goddaughter thought she had been "spoilt by adulation & hardened a little perhaps by controversy and abuse," but she also recalled that More "amused me more, & let me be more saucy than anybody else."[64]

In the third stanza of *Sanctified Knowledge*, a hymn of Charles Wesley, is the call to "Unite the pair so long disjoined;/Knowledge and vital piety."[65] And this is the very thing Hannah More's goddaughter recalled about the home of the More sisters: "Surely there never was such a house, so full of intellect and piety and active benevolence."[66] From what we know of that household its spiritual leader was Hannah More, who believed strongly that "a religion which is all brain, and no heart, is not the religion of the Gospel."[67] And so she told her readers: "I put religion on my right hand and learning on my left. Learning should not be despised even as an auxiliary."[68] But both hearts and minds needed to act in the world according to the

---

62. More, *Works*, ii., 309.

63. *Christian Observer* 33 (1833), 632.

64. Stott, *Hannah More*, p. ix.

65. Wesley and Wesley, *Poetical Works*, vi., 408.

66. Stott, *Hannah More*, 291.

67. More, *Works*, iii., 156.

68. Jones, *Hannah More*, 233.

gospel: "Search the Scriptures, seek the help of the Holy Spirit, follow Christ's example in well-doing and stretch every faculty in the service of the Lord."[69]

Between 1813 and 1819 Hannah More's four sisters died, as did many of her closest friends. But now well into middle age she made new, younger friends and, in addition to writing eleven books after she was sixty, kept up a social calendar that would have exhausted a teenager: in her eighties she wrote Wilberforce, "I saw fifty persons last week and it is commonly the same every week."[70] She was that rare person of her own or any time, one who wrote for and mixed in the fashionable world of a great city like London and the poor of the countryside. In her diary she mentions that one Thursday she dined with a bishop and the following Sunday with two miners. In spite of overwork and persistent ill health Hannah More lived on into her eighty-eighth year, passing away in 1833—six weeks after her beloved friend Wilberforce—leaving her very large fortune earned from writing to charities and religious societies.

With other members of the British elite of her time More shared the belief that social distinctions were mostly fixed—as well as part of God's plan. But she also emphasized the duty of those in middle and upper classes toward the less well off—making their lives better physically and helping them realize how fortunate they really were. This had the ironic effect of empowering them to change their lives for the better, thus changing their place in society and changing society itself. Paradoxically, this quite anti-revolutionary woman expressed thinking that was far more progressive than her most Enlightened contemporaries:

> At least, till the female sex are more carefully instructed, this question will always remain as undecided to the degree of difference between the masculine and feminine understanding, as the question between the understanding of blacks and whites; for until men and women, as well as Africans and Europeans, are put more nearly on a par in the cultivation of their minds, the shades of distinction, whatever they be, between their native abilities, can never be fairly ascertained.[71]

It would be audacious to suggest that one believing woman, a conservative and conventional one at that, saved her country from the ravages of

69. Ibid., 234.
70. Roberts, *Memoirs*, ii., 399.
71. More, *Works*, i., 367–68.

revolution, established the necessity for educating the masses and for a system of welfare, and was in effect the first feminist. But think about it. In helping preserve the social and political order, in the long run she in fact contributed to the evolution of democracy. In opening those sixteen schools she helped establish the principle of popular education. Her strong belief that humans can change both trickled down and flowed upwards. Her endeavors for and writing about females called for changing the situation of women from passive objects to active members of society.

Hannah More was a political conservative who campaigned for what were understood by some as revolutionary changes, an Anglican who attended a Presbyterian church, hired Methodists to teach for her, and praised Quakers; she has Jack in *Village Politics* argue, "I'd scorn to live in a country where there was not liberty of conscience; and where every man might not worship God his own way."[72] Her writings and philanthropic activities deeply influenced the public mind and social character of her day, evident in the letters and memoirs of her contemporaries. As we ponder More's life, think about how essential it is that Christians not abandon culture for their own safety or tranquility, but challenge it head on. That's what More did. Must we not do the same?

Her text

To maintain a devotional spirit two things are especially necessary; habitually to cultivate the disposition, and habitually to avoid whatever is unfavorable to it. Frequent retirement and recollection are indispensable together with such a general course of reading, as, if it does not actually promote the spirit we are endeavoring to maintain, shall never be hostile to it. . . .

These works [which were "prejudicial to moral and mental improvement"], if comparatively harmless, yet debase the taste, slacken the intellectual nerve, let down the understanding, set the imagination loose, and send it gadding among low and worthless objects. They not only run away with the time which should be given to better things, but gradually destroy all taste for better things. They sink the mind to their own standard, and give it a sluggish reluctance, we had almost said a moral incapacity, for every thing above their level. The mind, by long habit of stooping, loses its erectness, and yields to its degradation. It becomes so low and narrow by the littleness of the things which engage it, that it requires a painful effort

---

72. Ibid., i, 61.

to lift itself high enough, or to open itself wide enough, to embrace great and noble objects. The appetite is vitiated. Excess, instead of producing a surfeit by weakening the digestion, only induces a loathing for stronger nourishment. The faculties which might have been expanding in works of science, or soaring in the contemplation of genius, become satisfied with the impertinences of the most ordinary fiction, lose their relish for the severity of truth, the elegance of taste, and the soberness of religion. Lulled in the torpor of repose, the intellect dozes, and enjoys, in its waking dream, "All the wild trash of sleep without its rest."

In avoiding books which excite the passions, it would seem strange to include even some devotional works. Yet such as merely kindle warm feelings are not always the safest. Let us rather prefer those which, while they tend to raise a devotional spirit, awaken the affections without disordering them; which, while they elevate the desires, purify them; which show us our own nature, and lay open its corruptions. Such as show us the malignity of sin, the deceitfulness of our hearts, the feebleness of our best resolutions; such as teach us to pull off the mask from the fairest appearances, and discover every hiding place where some lurking evil would conceal itself; such as show us not what we appear to others, but what we really are; such as, cooperating with our interior feelings, and showing us our natural state, point out our absolute need of a Redeemer, lead us to seek to him for pardon, from a conviction that there is no other refuge, no other salvation. Let us be conversant with such writings as teach us that, while we long to obtain the remission of our transgressions, we must not desire the remission of our duties. Let us seek for such a Savior as will not only deliver us from the punishment of sin, but from its dominion also. . . .

If God be the center to which our hearts are tending, every line in our lives must meet in him. With this point in view, there will be a harmony between our prayers and our practice, a consistency between devotion and conduct which will make every part turn to this one end, bear upon this one point. For the beauty of the Christian scheme consists not in parts (however good in themselves) which tend to separate views and lead to different ends; but it arises from its being one entire, uniform, connected plan, "compacted of that which every joint supplies," and of which all the parts terminate in this one grand ultimate point.

Hannah More, *Practical Piety* (1811)

Questions

1. "Affliction is the school in which great virtues are acquired, in which great characters are formed." What stands out to you about how Hannah More responded to adversities and moments of crisis?

2. "Action is the life of virtue, and the world is the theatre of action." Given her story, what might More have meant by this saying in regard to her calling? In this regard, how did her calling evolve?

3. "The mischief arises not from our living in the world, but from the world living in us; occupying our hearts, and monopolizing our affections." How did More practice what she preached?

4. What role did encouragers play in More's life, in particular how and when she should proceed?

5. Did reading Hannah More's story provide you any insight into your own calling?

For further reading

Collingwood, Jeremy and Margaret Collingwood. *Hannah More.* Oxford: Lion, 1990.

Jones, Mary Gwladys. *Hannah More.* Cambridge: Cambridge University Press, 1952.

More, Hannah. *Works.* Online: http://www.gutenberg.org/browse/authors/m#a5807.

Stott, Anne. *Hannah More: The First Victorian.* Oxford: Oxford University Press, 2003.

CHAPTER 4

William Wilberforce

Story: Persuasion and Action

> True Christians . . . are not their own.
> William Wilberforce, aged 37

ON THE 24TH OF February, 1791, a tired eighty-eight-year-old wrote William Wilberforce, then a thirty-two-year-old British politician and anti-slavery campaigner:

> Unless God has raised you up . . . I see not how you can go through
> with your glorious enterprise in opposing that execrable villainy,
> which is the scandal of religion, of England, and of human nature.
> Unless God has raised you up for this very thing, you will be worn
> out by the opposition of men and devils; but if God is with you,
> who can be against you? Oh, be not weary in well-doing. Go on, in
> the name of God and in the power of his might, till even American
> slavery, the vilest that ever saw the sun, shall vanish away before
> it.[1]

It was the last letter John Wesley would ever write, for he died six days later. While never in a position to rid America of slavery, Wilberforce engaged his own nation powerfully, challenging his countrymen to reconsider their moral environment. He was a brilliant public campaigner, whose words and

---

1. Wesley, *Letters*, viii., 265.

deeds helped create a new dimension to how Britons perceived themselves, their society, and Britain's true national interest.

Wesley's letter prompts some questions: How did a young, wealthy, ambitious politician who might have eventually become Britain's prime minister choose instead a very different path, and what difference did that decision make—to him, his nation, and the world? What might the answers to those questions teach us, now over two centuries later, about what a thoughtful life given to God might produce? How is William Wilberforce a model of prudence—that is, what actions should one take, and when should they be taken?

William Wilberforce was born in 1759 in Hull, a port city in the north of England. His father, a prosperous merchant, died when he was nine and for a time Wilberforce was brought up by an uncle and aunt who lived in London and who were strong supporters of John Wesley and the Methodists. They took him to their evangelical Anglican parish church, where among various guest speakers Wilberforce heard John Newton. Formerly the captain of a slave ship, after his conversion Newton had become an Anglican priest, hymn writer, and spiritual counselor. Disturbed by what she heard was happening in her son's life, Mrs. Wilberforce, a nominal Christian, brought William back home to in effect reprogram him.

When he was seventeen Wilberforce entered Cambridge University, and soon inherited even more wealth with the deaths of his grandfather and an uncle—making him by today's standards a millionaire many times over. He recalled his beginning days at Cambridge: "I was introduced . . . on the very first night of my arrival, to as licentious a set of men as can well be conceived. They drank hard, and their conversation was even worse than their lives."[2] Those words also fit their author, for while at the university Wilberforce studied little, gambled and drank a lot, and earned a reputation for wit and eloquence. It was at Cambridge that Wilberforce began a life-long friendship with William Pitt the younger, the future prime minister.

In 1780, Wilberforce stood for election to the House of Commons for Hull, and after expending a great deal of money at the ripe old age of twenty-one, he won. Though not a landowner or from a noble family, four years later he was elected for the county of Yorkshire which, because the number of voters was the largest in the land, conferred a greater power and significance. Still only in his mid-twenties, Wilberforce had dazzling prospects before him. In an era of outstanding political orators Pitt paid

---

2. Wilberforce and Wilberforce, *Life*, i., 10.

him the rare compliment that he had "the greatest natural eloquence of all the men I ever met."[3] Wilberforce's wit drew others to him; his independent stance signaled a willingness to put principles over party. And as he put it, "I was then very ambitious."[4]

Wilberforce's early years in Parliament were typical for rich, ruthless young men. Noted for both confidence and charm, attributes no doubt enhanced by his considerable wealth, he was playing at politics, not involving himself with any great cause. Wilberforce continued his gambling and excessive drinking, and now agreed with enlightened British public opinion that Methodists were vulgar and ignorant. While in London he attended a Unitarian chapel, later commenting that by then he had "imbibed skeptical notions."[5] Whatever spiritual progress had been made during his stay with his uncle and aunt was now in retreat, Wilberforce applauding the Unitarian preacher as "more earnest and practical than others."[6]

Wilberforce later described his then state, his "darling object"[7] as he put it, as centered on himself: "Emulation, and a desire of distinction, were my governing motives; and ardent after the applause of my fellow-creatures, I quite forgot that I was an accountable being."[8] Driven by ambition, his great gift of eloquence was used to destroy opponents in parliamentary debates—including at one point Lord North, then prime minister—with whom he was at odds over the government's war with the rebellious American colonies. As the closest political friend and confidante of Pitt, who in 1784 became prime minister, Wilberforce was at the center of power of the world's most powerful nation. But a year after his Yorkshire election Wilberforce had an experience which completely changed his outlook and behavior.

Conversion

The turning point in his life began during a vacation in the south of France. He asked a fellow Yorkshireman and brilliant Cambridge professor, the younger brother of his former schoolteacher, to be his companion—not

3. Tomkins, *Wilberforce*, 29.

4. Harford, *Recollections*, 203.

5. Ibid., 206.

6. Wilberforce and Wilberforce, *Life*, i., 76.

7. Ibid., i., 149.

8. Ibid., i., 28.

knowing that the man was an evangelical Christian, later commenting in words that all believers can echo that God "blesses us not only without, but even against, our own plans and inclinations."[9] Wilberforce spent the first part of the trip ridiculing evangelicals. In the luggage of his traveling companion he saw a book, *The Rise and Progress of Religion in the Soul*, written by a widely-read Congregationalist minister, Philip Doddridge. When he asked his friend about it, he was informed that this was "one of the best books ever written."[10] The two of them agreed to read it together on the journey, and Wilberforce was so moved by being introduced to the intellectual heart of Christianity that he began reading the New Testament in Greek.

The consequence was turmoil: he discovered that "my feelings too little corresponded with the convictions of my understanding,"[11] and while convicted about his lifestyle and ambition he was loath to give them up. "As soon as I reflected seriously upon these subjects," he noted in his diary, "the deep guilt and black ingratitude of my past life forced itself upon me in the strongest colors, and I condemned myself for having wasted my precious time, and opportunities, and talents."[12] As he played at politics so he played at religion: attending church, observers might have thought he was a believer, but his behavior was not matched by beliefs.

As the events of his conversion were unfolding he poured out his soul to his sister, writing that "There is no opinion so fatal as that which is commonly received in these liberal days, that a person is in a safe state with respect to a future world, if he acts tolerably up to his knowledge and convictions, though he may not have taken much pains about acquiring this knowledge or fixing these convictions."[13] Those convictions included the offer of the gospel as free and universal, and that he needed to ask God to receive the Holy Spirit. And so, as he put it, "such thoughts as these completely occupied my mind, and I began to pray earnestly."[14] In despair concerning his state Wilberforce turned to the sixty-year-old Newton, who initiated a process which led him to recognize that wealth, power, and ambition are insufficient to build a life upon, and so he came to Christ.

9. Ibid., i., 75.

10. Ibid., i., 76.

11. Harford, *Recollections*, 211.

12. Wilberforce and Wilberforce, *Life*, i., 88.

13. Ibid., i., 73.

14. Ibid., i., 88.

His conversion was, as he would testify, not to dogma, not to religion, not to the church but to Jesus. Henceforth Wilberforce's winsome personality and eloquence were carried over to new efforts leading, motivating, and cooperating with others, his earnestness now tempered by humility. Modesty replaced blind ambition. When working on some goal with those who had rejected Christianity he never came across as defensive or sanctimonious, combining spiritual depth with charm, friendly demeanor, and perseverance. In fact, according to James Macintosh, a fellow parliamentarian who was an atheist and politically far more radical than Wilberforce, "I never saw anyone who touched life at so many points and this is the more remarkable in a man who is supposed to live absorbed in the contemplation of a future state. When he was in the House of Commons he seemed to have the freshest mind of any man there."[15] Would political opponents and atheists say that of believers today?

Wilberforce's encounter with Christ was the fulcrum of his personal and public life. His spiritual crisis—as he put it, a "state of the deepest depression"[16]—went on for seventeen months, during which he read everything he could get his hands on until at Easter in 1786 he had "a settled conviction in my mind, not only of the truth of Christianity, but also of the scriptural basis of the leading doctrines which I now hold."[17] "I seem to myself to have awakened about nine or ten years ago from a dream," Wilberforce put the change a decade later, "to have recovered, as it were, the use of my reason after a delirium."[18] He thereupon resigned from his five fashionable clubs, renounced gambling, and found himself fired with a passion for learning he never had at school or university. In the years that followed Wilberforce sought to make up for the years he had wasted by an intense regimen of reading and reflection; he spent nine to ten hours per day reading the Bible and his era's best minds, whether fiction or social and political thought. To achieve this he had to carve out time from what had been the dinner parties and other gatherings where much of the work of the politician is done. Wilberforce understood that if he were to be God's politician he must redeem his time, writing in his diary that such occasions "disqualified me for every useful purpose in life, waste my time, impair my health, fill my mind with thoughts of resistance before and self-condemna-

15. Ibid., v., 315–16.

16. Ibid., i., 89.

17. Harford, *Recollections*, 208.

18. Wilberforce and Wilberforce, *Life*, i., 107.

tion afterwards."[19] Even in his first years as a believer Wilberforce realized his life was not his own.

Calling

Withdrawing for a season of prayer and reflection on his vocation, Wilberforce considered a career change, including becoming a clergyman, but was persuaded by Newton that his calling was to serve God through politics, "that the Lord has raised you up for the good of the nation."[20] Interestingly, although his friend Pitt was not a believer he concurred with Newton's advice. After Wilberforce's conversion Pitt asked him: "If a Christian may act in the several relations of life, must he exclude himself from all to become so? Surely the principles as well as the practice of Christianity are simple, and lead not to mediation only, but to action."[21] And so Wilberforce entered in his diary: "My walk is a public one. My business is in the world; and I must mix in the assemblies of men, or quit the post which Providence seems to have assigned me."[22] Soon thereafter he leased a house across the street from where Parliament met: politics was to be his world, or perhaps more to the point his parish.

The public walk, the mixing in the assemblies of men may look secular, but was as spiritual—perhaps in his case more so—than had he become a pastor. Contemporaries dubbed Wilberforce and his allies "the Saints," recognizing, not always in a complimentary fashion, that the motivation for their actions lay beyond political office or power for its own sake. Thus when Wilberforce stood on the floor of the House of Commons, he was on holy ground. Signifying his own sense that politics was his vocation, he set the highest standard for himself: "A man who acts from the principles I profess reflects that he is to give an account of his political conduct at the judgment seat of Christ."[23] Accountability became one of the hallmarks of his public life.

We see Wilberforce's calling from a diary entry on October 28, 1787: "God almighty has set before me two great objects, the suppression of the

19. Hague, *Wilberforce*, 101.
20. Wilberforce and Wilberforce, *Correspondence*, i., 56.
21. Wilberforce, *Private Papers*, 13.
22. Wilberforce and Wilberforce, *Life*, i., 187.
23. Hancock, "'Shrimp' Who Stopped Slavery," 15.

Slave Trade and the Reformation of Manners [morals]."[24] He was only twenty-eight when he became the leader of the effort in Parliament to abolish the slave trade and simultaneously labored to encourage a return to civility and human flourishing in British life. But before discussing how he sought to act on his calling, his "two great objects," let's look first at the springs in Wilberforce's life that provided resources for his remarkable achievements, for these means were as astonishing as the ends.

The first of these springs combined friendship, community, and accountability. Early in his walk as a believer Wilberforce learned the value of close friends to whom he might open his heart and who in private confronted him regarding his faults. A network of such friends meant that the whole was greater than the sum of its parts: collectively Wilberforce and others could achieve far more than would have been the case with isolated individuals. He advised one of his sons: "[Bring] together all men who are like-minded, and may one day combine and concert for the public good. Never omit any opportunity, my dear Samuel, of getting acquainted with any good or useful man."[25]

Along with others Wilberforce established a model for a family-centered lifestyle and neighborliness. In 1792 he began sharing a home with his cousin, Henry Thornton, in Clapham, just south of London. After both men married Wilberforce leased and finally bought a house there, where he lived until 1808. In turn many of his friends moved to be near him. Others like Hannah More were frequent visitors to Clapham down until 1815 when death and departure broke up this experiment in intimate Christian community. The network of Christian activists later called—sometimes with contempt—the Clapham Sect, was a brotherhood of a dozen evangelical members of the Church of England—politicians, bankers, government administrators, lawyers, diplomats, businessmen, and wealthy philanthropists. Their mentor was John Venn, rector of Holy Trinity church, Clapham. For four decades Clapham was the Rome and Harvard of British evangelicalism. The Clapham brotherhood was able to support one another in applying their faith to public service because of the depth of their spiritual and intellectual fellowship. Friendship combined with Christian community produced accountability, which was critical for the perseverance of the saints.

24. Wilberforce and Wilberforce, *Life*, i., 149.
25. Ibid., i., 184.

When American president Thomas Jefferson asked Wilberforce what the Clapham circle represented, Wilberforce wrote back using a memorable phrase, a "concert of benevolence."[26] Wilberforce's second distinctive characteristic then was his philanthropy. The son of one member of the Clapham sect believed that Wilberforce had an "instinct of philanthropy."[27] Hence it was that until his later thirties, when he married, each year he gave away one fourth of his income. His principle, in his own words, was that, "When summoned to give an account of our stewardship, we shall be called upon to answer for the use we have made of relieving the wants and necessities of our fellow creatures."[28] Thus it was that he founded or contributed significantly to nearly seventy organizations, what we would today term NGOs and non-profits. Many of his charitable activities were done in conjunction with the Clapham brotherhood.

The third source of what Wilberforce was able to accomplish was his writing. Do you believe in the power of ideas to change society? Wilberforce and his friends certainly did, or they would never have taken so much time away from their business, public affairs, and families to write so many books, pamphlets, and articles in magazines. Even though he was an exceptionally active politician in and out of parliament Wilberforce carved out time to pen the 350-page *Practical View of the Prevailing Religious System of Professed Christians in the Higher and Middle Classes in this Country, Contrasted with Real Christianity*, which he published in 1797 after working on it for several years; it remained a best-seller for four decades. The book reflected the author's spiritual journey from doubt to deep, personal faith in Jesus, contrasting nominal with vibrant Christianity—the former engendering despair, the latter hope.

In Wilberforce's mind the book set out the virtues which best signify how holy our lives are actually capable of being: "the fear and love of God and of Christ[;] love, kindness, and meekness towards our fellow-creatures[;] indifference to the possessions and events of this life, in comparison with our concern about eternal things[;] self-denial and humility."[29] If the teachings of Jesus as put forth in the Bible were true, lives must be completely informed by them. Therefore Wilberforce counseled:

---

26. Ibid., iii., 374.
27. Belmonte, *Hero for Humanity*, 240.
28. Wilberforce, *Practical View*, 5.
29. Ibid., 198.

> Let your love be more affectionate, your mildness less open to irritation . . . Consider sweetness of temper and activity of mind, if they naturally belong to you, as talents of special worth and utility, for which you will have to give account. . . . keep them in continual exercise, and direct them to their noblest ends.[30]

To accomplish this, his advice was simple: take the Bible off the shelf, open it up and "imbibe the principles, and practice the precepts of Christ."[31]

In 1802 Wilberforce helped found the *Christian Observer*, a monthly magazine, and from that year onward helped ensure it was must reading for believers concerned with thinking Christianly about the era's most important social and political questions. We should also note his *Letter on the Abolition of the Slave Trade, Addressed to the Freeholders and Other Inhabitants of Yorkshire* (1807), where in 400 pages Wilberforce marshaled the evidence he had collected since he began his efforts in support of the abolition campaign. The *Letter on the Abolition of the Slave Trade* included these powerful lines, penned for his fellow believers:

> [I]f the Slave Trade be a national crime, . . . to which we cling in defiance of the clearest light, not only in opposition to our own acknowledgments of its guilt, but even of our own declared resolutions to abandon it; is not this then a time in which all who are not perfectly sure that the Providence of God is but a fable, should be strenuous in their endeavours to lighten the vessel of the state, of such a load of guilt and infamy?[32]

The fourth spring of Wilberforce's life was his independence. That he approached politics from a moral stance was evident when he risked a break with his friend Pitt over continuing the war against France that had begun in the early 1790s. Regarding his country Wilberforce had written in *Practical View of Professed Christians Contrasted with Real Christianity*: "I must confess . . . that my only solid hopes for the well-being of my country depend, not so much on her fleets and armies, not so much on the wisdom of her rulers or the spirit of her people, as on the persuasion that she still contains many who love and obey the gospel of Christ."[33] Putting words into practice in 1794 on the floor of the House of Commons, Wilberforce offered an amendment urging Pitt's government to pursue peace, and in the

30. Ibid., 201.
31. Ibid., 6.
32. Wilberforce, *Letter on the Slave Trade*, 5–6.
33. Wilberforce, *Practical View*, 274.

next year supported an opposition motion to the same end. Both actions deeply hurt Pitt, but their friendship endured because the prime minister understood Wilberforce's efforts grew out of what he understood as God's leading—which Wilberforce implied when in his speech he stated that he had been elected to parliament "to discharge a great political trust; and for the faithful administration of the power vested in me, I must answer to my country and my God."[34]

Was William Wilberforce a Christian politician? Certainly he was—but of an all-too infrequent type. Recently a contemporary British historian who is as well a leading political figure made the important observation that "his influence stemmed not only from his belief but from his quality of mind."[35] Wilberforce spent many hours every week over a course of years researching his causes, looking at them from multiple angles, thinking about and writing—and rewriting—his several books. It was only after his conversion that he became very serious about the life of mind, and that seriousness shaped his political life—as more than one observer noted.

Something of this seriousness is evident in a print based on an 1801 portrait that combines elements of the debater, the author, and the activist, displaying for the world to see what defined his character—persuasion and action. The original portrait was actually painted six years *before* the end of the slave trade, when Wilberforce was forty-one. It reflects the optimism in the poet William Cowper's 1792 *Sonnet to William Wilberforce*:

William Wilberforce
By James Heath, after John Russell
© National Portrait Gallery, London

> Fear not lest labour such as thine be vain!
> Thou hast achiev'd a part; hast gain'd the ear
> Of Britain's senate to thy glorious cause;
> Hope smiles, joy springs, and tho' cold caution pause
> And weave delay, the better hour is near.[36]

In the portrait the sitter looks hopefully at viewer, holding the "Slave Trade Abolition Bill." Beyond him lies a volume of [*Parliamentary*] *Debates* and another volume, *Parliamentary Register*,

34. Wilberforce and Wilberforce, *Life*, i., 90–91.

35. Cormack, *Wilberforce*, 121.

36. Cowper, *Minor Poems*, 48.

as if to ask the viewer, "Will you join me in translating biblical truth into political action to protect the least of these?"

Achievements

Four great consequences of Wilberforce's conversion, calling, and character stand out, all of which were connected: abolishing the slave trade, initiating a moral reformation within British society, reconceptualizing the relationship between Europe and Africa, and ending slavery in Britain's empire.

As already evident in the discussion of Olaudah Equiano, slaves were abducted from west Africa, transported by ship to the Americas, and exchanged for goods that were conveyed to Britain. Most well-informed Britons thought the trade necessary if nasty, economically vital as a source of inexpensive labor on sugar plantations in the Caribbean. Slaves were considered private property, and thus prior to Wilberforce's campaign slavery was understood to be an economic not a moral issue. Britain was the world's leader in the trade, and had by Wilberforce's time supplied three million slaves to French, Spanish, and British colonies. While for quite some time my fellow historians argued that slavery was abolished when it was no longer profitable, the best sources now available suggest the opposite, that in fact when abolition came the slave trade was still quite lucrative. Therefore we now need to scrutinize Wilberforce's exploits more carefully than we would have had to do a few years ago.

After looking over the facts a friend had amassed against the trade Wilberforce became the most prominent public face of the anti-slavery movement. As he read the evidence he became horrified—at the state of slaves, at the harm being done to Africa, at the conditions of the slave trade, especially the high death rate during the Atlantic crossing. He resolved to give the abolition movement his personal support—no matter the consequences for his political prospects. He was then convinced by an evangelical couple to introduce a bill in parliament that would outlaw the trade. The anti-slavery effort was the first of the great national campaigns that helped reshape Britain into a democracy, more than a century before parliament enacted one person, one vote.

Wilberforce introduced his first anti-slavery motion in the House of Commons in 1789. His nearly four-hour oration appealed to both the hearts and heads of his fellow parliamentarians, and by extension the nation. Through his speech Wilberforce brought his audience on to a slave

ship and allowed them to imagine the horrors of the middle passage, expos-
ing the inhumanity of those engaged in the trade and the deceit employed
on the part of their defenders. Wilberforce followed by presenting evidence
to support a terrible statistic: fully half the slaves kidnapped in Africa died
before they were ready to work in the New World. "We are all guilty," Wilberforce argued, "we all ought to plead guilty." And he concluded with these
thoughts:

> The nature and all the circumstances of the Trade are now laid
> open to us. We can no longer plead ignorance . . . we cannot turn
> aside so as to avoid seeing it . . . Let us make reparation to Africa,
> as far as we can, by establishing trade upon true commercial prin-
> ciples . . . [W]hen we think of eternity and the future consequence
> of all human conduct, what is there in this life that shall make
> any man contradict the dictates of his conscience, the principles of
> justice and the law of God![37]

A masterpiece of parliamentary oratory—one newspaper termed it "one
the best speeches ever delivered in Parliament"[38]—the motion was nevertheless defeated. Wilberforce had been overly confident in the rightness
of his cause, having "no doubt of our success."[39] But just because a case is
compelling doesn't mean it will inevitably push out what is false. In this
instance, the rising secular worldview of laissez-faire and the vested economic interests at home and abroad that supported slavery trumped Christian moral thinking. Then, and we have all heard it in our own time, the
prevailing argument was that to be competitive the nation could not afford
to put morality ahead of economics. Consequently, between 1791 and 1800
the slave trade actually increased.

Most of Wilberforce's political allies in Parliament were opposed to
any restrictions on the slave trade and at first he had to rely on the support of his political opponents, which, of course, was never going to move
him forward politically. In fact, further advancement in his political career
was now ended, because the one thing politicians rarely forgive is putting
principles ahead of party. While in the future his fellow parliamentarians
may have paid lip service to Wilberforce's virtuous behavior, any aspiration
he had ever had to climb the political ladder was gone for good. In essence,

37. Cobbett, *Parliamentary History of England*, xxviii., 63.

38. *General Evening Post*, May 12–14, 1789.

39. Hague, *Life*, 142.

ambition had given way to antagonizing the very men prepared to reward him with power.

For eighteen years Wilberforce introduced anti-slavery motions in Parliament. A self-confessed melancholic, in spite of failure he nevertheless persisted. When war, the rhetoric of vested interests, and slave rebellions in French colonies hardened attitudes toward abolition, Wilberforce pressed on, collecting petitions signed by hundreds of thousands of Britons, holding meetings, publishing pamphlets, and helping to organize a boycott of slave-produced sugar. Twice he was physically assaulted, and twice challenged to a duel. He was for a time the most vilified man in Britain, despised by most of the nation's powerful people, some of whom accused him of being as bad as the French revolutionaries. Admiral Nelson, Britain's greatest naval hero, wrote that as long as he could speak he would resist "the damnable doctrines of Wilberforce and his hypocritical allies."[40]

But what Nelson missed the great American abolitionist Frederick Douglass later saw—that in spite of political setbacks Wilberforce and his allies had "thawed the British heart,"[41] that in the words of one historian of British imperialism, "it might be said that the moral transformation of the British empire began in Holy Trinity church in Clapham."[42] And so it was that finally all the years of effort combined with creative tactics and public relations campaigns bore fruit in 1807 when the House of Commons voted overwhelmingly to abolish the slave trade. Members of Parliament turned to Wilberforce and began cheering. Wilberforce sat, head bowed, tears streaming down his face as the bill passed. By persisting in the face of adversity—including the deaths of William Pitt the year before and John Newton that year—Wilberforce, once reviled, had become the living embodiment of the national conscience. For perhaps the first time in history a nation turned its back on what had been believed to be its economic self-interest in favor of doing what was right.

Can a culture be won back? The outcome of Wilberforce's efforts in his second great cause is less measurable and more limited than enthusiasts suggest the evidence points to, for the endeavor was even more daunting than abolishing the profitable slave trade. It is Jesus who permanently changes cultures—one heart and one mind at a time. But it is equally true that Wilberforce's effort was extraordinary, for in many ways he and his

40. Knutsford, *Life and Letters of Macaulay*, 258.
41. Belmonte, *Hero for Humanity*, 19.
42. Ferguson, *Empire*, 96.

allies both pioneered the modern pressure group and helped set the tone for the generation that followed.

As with his conversion, Wilberforce's efforts to promote moral reform began by reading a book on how nearly a century earlier a campaign had been carried out to eliminate public corruption by reviving religion. Very much behind the scenes in 1787, Wilberforce founded the Society for the Reformation of Manners, which aimed at restraining the growth of immorality and promoting civility—because he believed that manners matter. Wilberforce proposed doing this by challenging the trendsetters—in our times the types one sees in *People Magazine*, but back then the nobility, gentry, and bishops—to rethink how their behavior affected those who observed them. His approach was to travel around the country to win people over, for example by using "launchers," phrases he would interject at posh dinner parties to turn the talk to deeper matters.

Without their realizing Wilberforce was behind the Society, he got a good many prominent people to join. The point was never to *be religious*, and some who joined had at that moment no faith and the worst of lifestyles. The point was to take Britain down a different path than the one where, because coarseness and vulgarity flourished so did slavery and the brutalization of Africans as well as poor Britons. And so it was that he never let a teachable moment pass. Writing to one rising politician whose politics and faith were completely at odds with his own, Wilberforce closed his letter with an encouragement: "May the Almighty grant you a long Course of Usefulness and Honour, and may this be succeeded by a still better portion in a better World."[43]

Wilberforce believed laws were important for reducing temptations rather than changing the human heart. As his fellow Member of Parliament Edmund Burke put it, "Manners are of more importance than laws. Upon them, in a great measure, the laws depend."[44] For Wilberforce, saving society came only by salvation of individuals, "an absolute surrender of soul and body to the will and service of God."[45] As he wrote in *Practical View of Professed Christians Contrasted with Real Christianity*, "It is the true duty of every man to promote the happiness of his fellow creatures to the utmost of his power."[46] But he recognized in his own life that negative habits can

43. Kriegel, "Saints and Whigs," 428.
44. Burke, *First Letter on a Regicide Peace*, 242.
45. Wilberforce, *Practical View*, 248.
46. Ibid., ii.

be starved of nourishment and become dormant, just as positive habits can be fed. The greatest critics of his endeavor were secular-minded radicals, for Wilberforce preached that attempts at social reform without a spiritual base would create flawed programs and actually hurt the poor; the poor understood this point better than the critics. Others censured Wilberforce and his ally Hannah More for promoting alienation on the part of the poor against their social superiors.

Wilberforce practiced what he preached, growing more generous as time went on. Some of his contributions appear to have been directly connected to his faith. Thus he gave financial support to friends who worked to provide poor children with education in reading, personal hygiene, and religion. He helped launch the Bible Society and the Church Missionary Society. With two others he founded the Society for Bettering the Condition and Increasing the Comforts of the Poor, with practical schemes for soup kitchens, subsidized village shops, self-insurance societies, and nutritious recipes, all based on his belief that, "In proportion as we can multiply domestic comforts, in the same degree we may hope to promote the cause of morality and virtue."[47] Wilberforce was an early supporter of legal and religious equality for Catholics.

In other cases his legislative and organizational causes expanded beyond what in this era might have been predictable from his faith. He supported legislation to reform Britain's political system and was instrumental in getting a bill passed that reduced capital punishments. He sought to improve the conditions of chimney sweeps, soldiers and sailors, and prisoners, including prisoners of wars, to create more and better-managed hospitals, and to carry out reforms in the administration of the Indian colonies. He was a founder of the National Portrait Gallery and of the Royal Society for the Prevention of Cruelty to Animals—the world's first organization to protect animals.

It makes sense to connect what looks spiritual and what looks secular, taking both back to Wilberforce's understanding of his calling—"my business is in the world."[48] Perhaps the best way to measure his influence in reforming manners is to observe the children of the people he affected. In this sense the Victorian generation was far different in religion and lifestyle than its parents, and that's quite a legacy—even if he did not do it all by

47. Society for Bettering the Condition and Increasing the Comforts of the Poor, *Reports*, i., 263.

48. Wilberforce and Wilberforce, *Life*, i., 187.

himself, and even if it didn't last, because we're only responsible for our own times.

This was true as well of his efforts for Africans. Wilberforce was a co-founder of the Sierra Leone Company, whose mission was to resettle freed slaves and promote trade with west Africa, and the African Institution, which sought to collect information on the slave trade carried out by other nations—especially the United States—and to promote development in west Africa. In the late eighteenth century a consortium of London businessmen had carried out a very profitable slaving venture in Sierra Leone. Reclaiming that territory for normal trade and farming combined with the end of the slave trade would go some way toward recognizing the humanness of Africans while at the same time helping atone for British slavery.

The efforts of the "friends of Africa," as they were termed, were visible in three areas. The response of a number of Manchester manufacturers to the abolition movement was that ending the slave trade would ruin them because they produced the goods traded for slaves, and thus in turn would their workers be impoverished. Second, particularly among well-educated Britons there was a strongly held belief that Africans were racially inferior to Europeans, and thus they could only progress within slavery. Finally, some Christians argued that slavery was an opportunity for conversion of the mostly animist Africans. Wilberforce and allies used the familiarity of Britons with such interchanges about Africa and its inhabitants to challenge each of these arguments.

Wilberforce taught the members of the House of Commons that Africans had a "genius for commerce,"[49] and on other occasions pressed his listeners and readers to understand that were trade on an equal footing both Britain and Africa would prosper. The Sierra Leone colony, with all its problems, saw whites, indigenous Africans, and repatriated ex-slaves and blacks who had fought on the British side against the American revolutionaries live on terms of equality—which, while not fatally undermining the racial myths, provided data to contradict them. That slavery was a betrayal of Christianity was a centerpiece of every campaign that Wilberforce waged, and was countered by the successful export of the Countess of Huntington's churches to Africa that we saw in the first chapter. With other friends of Africa Wilberforce demonstrated to a nation that was now prepared to listen to them that if free, Africans would flourish. And with truly remarkable foresight Wilberforce warned about the negative consequences arising out

49. Wilberforce, *Letter on the Slave Trade,* 370.

of racial animosities in southern Africa, suggesting he was a century and a half ahead of the rest of his country.

After decades of work having triumphed in ending the slave trade in 1807 one would have expected Wilberforce to pull back—but he didn't. Wilberforce and his allies had deceived themselves about how changing the law would lead to the demise of the institution of slavery, for the planters failed to emancipate their slaves. Thus his last campaign was against slavery itself. Back in 1807 Wilberforce was convinced as Equiano had been before him that the institution of slavery should be entirely abolished, but understood that there was little political will for emancipation.

By the 1820s, Wilberforce's health, never good, was deteriorating. He was unable to campaign with the same vigor that he used for the abolition of the slave trade. However, he continued to attack slavery both at public meetings and in the House of Commons. In 1823, he published an important anti-slavery pamphlet. *An Appeal to the Religion, Justice and Humanity of the Inhabitants of the British Empire on Behalf of the Negro Slaves in the West Indies* was connected to the foundation of the Anti-Slavery Society, which led the campaign to emancipate all slaves in the British empire. Leadership of the parliamentary campaign, however, passed from Wilberforce to others. In very poor health in 1825—likely in part from his decades of using opium to relieve intense pain—at age sixty-five Wilberforce resigned from the House of Commons after serving there for forty-five years. But he kept at the cause.

His last public appearance, at age seventy-one, was at a meeting in 1830 of the Anti-Slavery Society. In Parliament, the Emancipation Bill gathered support, and Wilberforce received word on July 26, 1833 that actions in the House of Commons pointed to its final passage. Three days later he was dead. Within a year, 800,000 slaves, chiefly in the British Caribbean colonies, became free. Wilberforce had helped to lead his generation to imagine something which had not existed for thousands of years—a world without slaves.

There are five lessons we might learn from the life and efforts of William Wilberforce. Mere believers today would do well to imitate each of the five—whatever our situation.

First, following his conversion as he grew older Wilberforce's sense of calling grew deeper and deeper—despite discouragements. The deeper the sense of calling, the more focused his attention span. Even in the midst of depression, even in defeat in 1796 Wilberforce could note in his diary, "being providentially engaged in [defeating] the slave trade business."[50] And this even though almost all his work took place in secular realms where he was open to criticism, even physical attack. And even though he was never in good health: in 1788 he almost died from an intestinal infection; he may have had not one but two nervous breakdowns; in the last two decades of his life he suffered from curvature of the spine so severe that he had to wear a metal brace, and he used opium daily to relieve the pain—while experiencing the side effect of depression; and a problem with his lungs led to his 1825 retirement from parliament. And even though one child died, and another so squandered his fortune that at the end of his life Wilberforce and his wife gave up their home, residing with the couple's younger sons. Nonetheless, he maintained his integrity in an age where for the well-to-do that virtue was in short supply.

A second lesson evident in Wilberforce's life was his biblical rootedness combined with a deep, personal faith in Christ. He was willing to pay the price for his politics because he knew Christ had paid the ultimate price for Wilberforce. From this realization came patience and perseverance: that moral ideas and a sustained campaign have the potential to change a culture. Wilberforce was a reader of the Word who was also a doer of the Word. Pay close attention to what characterized his Christian walk: daily devotions in the very early morning and evening, including self reflection, time spent in nature, Bible reading, prayer (his goal was an hour per day), and considering the signs of providence. This led him to conclude that, "I always find that I have the most time for business, and it is best done, when I have most properly observed my private devotions,"[51] a philosophy he picked up from Doddridge's *Rise and Progress of Religion*.

The third lesson, to repeat a theme, was the importance of teamwork when striving toward specific ends. Wilberforce's calling was as much corporate as individual. His living communally in the middle of his life—not so much like the 1960s but more like the sixties AD—fostered accountability, and was so unlike our own hyper-individualistic times. The Clapham brotherhood saved him from himself. As he put it in a diary entry, "Pride is my greatest stumbling block; and there is danger in it in two ways—lest it should make me desist from a Christian life, through fear of the world,

---

50. Wilberforce and Wilberforce, *Life*, i., 166.

51. Ibid., iii., 388.

my [pagan] friends, etc.; or if I persevere, lest it should make me vain of so doing."[52]

Fourth, Wilberforce's persuasion and action was out of the whole of his mind—which meant he was not a fanatic but a well-rounded human being. His causes were not who he was but grew out of whose he was. His friend Hannah More wrote regarding Wilberforce's wit that he had "as much as if he had no piety," while Maria, Lady Stanley having met him remarked, "Of all the lively entertaining men I ever saw, the Saint Wilberforce for me!"[53] Later in life Wilberforce wrote to another Christian politician about the deficit of delight among many of his fellow believers.

> My grand objection to the religious system still held by many who declare themselves orthodox Churchmen . . . is, that it tends to render Xianity so much a system of prohibitions rather than of privilege and hopes, and thus the injunction to rejoice so strongly enforced in the New Testament is practically neglected, and Religion is made to wear a forbidding and gloomy air and not one of peace and hope and joy.[54]

Wilberforce famously worked both sides of the aisle, telling the Speaker of the House of Commons his goal was "to promote the cordial and vigorous and systematic exertions of all . . . softening prejudices, healing divisions and striving to substitute a rational and an honest zeal for fundamentals in place of a hot party spirit."[55] As a politician who was a believer, Wilberforce was better at explaining what—and who—he was for than he was what—and who—he was against.

> Let Christians espouse that party in political life whose measures appear to them best adapted to produce public happiness; but let them be moderate in their political attachments. Let them love their fellow-citizens with a "pure heart, fervently;" considering their obligations to love and friendly sympathy, which are not to be dissolved by differences as to the characters of public men, or the issue of public measures.[56]

---

52. Ibid., i., 91–92.

53. Roberts, *Memoirs of Hannah More*, ii., 140–41; Adeane, *Maria Josepha, Lady Stanley*, 313.

54. Hague, *Life*, 100.

55. Pollock, *Wilberforce*, 153.

56. *Christian Observer* 1 (1802), 60.

Thus it was that Robert Southey, the Poet Laureate, lauded his public reputation: "the weight with which his opinion came to the public" was "far greater than [that] of any other individual."[57]

Finally, Wilberforce was uncompromising on principles, but flexible on tactics—hence the strategic partnerships that characterized his public career. He embodied the ubiquitous Christian maxim: "In things essential, unity. In things non-essential, liberty. And in all things, charity." Once again, such an attitude appears in sharp contrast to our own times. Should we not be saddened less by Christian leaders' peccadilloes—for don't we all struggle with something—than by words and tactics that might shame the most militant secular humanist? This was certainly the case with Wilberforce, who wrote to a close friend contrasting humility with pride, "the vice, which, in its essential nature and appropriate effects, is the most opposite to the genius and spirit of real Christianity."[58]

Wilberforce was buried in Westminster Abbey next to his friend William Pitt. A few years later a statue was erected there to a man who stood barely five feet four inches tall but who was one of his era's giants. If our measure is whether Britain was a genuinely Christian society in 1833 he failed. The better question to ask is, did Wilberforce along with fellow believers reshape how hundreds of thousands of Britons regarded themselves and their neighbors, and prove that society could be changed by doing it, thereby convincing those who followed that "the world would at length be moved"?[59] In that case, of whom else might it be said that the moral standards of a succeeding generation "were remarkably different from those of a generation before; a genuine advance in decency had occurred"[60]—and this from a critical historian.

What Wilberforce did was to put down a marker—for his own time. He did what Martin Luther asked all Christians to do—for their own time:

> If I profess with the loudest voice and clearest exposition every portion of the truth of God except precisely that little point that the world and the devil are at the moment attacking, I am not confessing Christ, however boldly I may be professing Christ, and to

---

57. Wilberforce and Wilberforce, *Life*, iv., 373.

58. Wilberforce, *Correspondence*, ii., 25.

59. Spring, "Clapham Sect," 40.

60. Hind, "Wilberforce and the British People," 325.

> be steady on all the battlefield besides is merely flight and disgrace if he flinches at that point.[61]

By William Wilberforce's death Britain had gone from being the leading slave trading nation in the world to the world's leader in opposing the trade. In the words of one leading historian of Wilberforce's era, "This had been an extraordinary revolution in sensibility and ideas."[62] A revolution indeed—as attested to by these lines on his statue in Westminster Abbey: "In an age and country fertile in great and good men, he was among the foremost of those who fixed the character of their times."[63]

---

61. Schaeffer, *God Who is There*, 18.
62. Colley, *Britons*, 351.
63. Furneaux, *William Wilberforce*, 456.

His text

I apprehend the essential practical characteristic of true Christians to be this: that relying on the promises to repenting sinners of acceptance through the Redeemer, they have renounced and abjured all other masters, and have cordially and unreservedly devoted themselves to God. . . . It is now their determined purpose to yield themselves without reserve to the reasonable service of the Rightful Sovereign. They are not their own: their bodily and mental faculties, their natural and acquired endowments, their substance, their authority, their time, their influence, all these they consider as belonging to them [should] be consecrated to the honor of God and employed in his service. . . .

The time is fast approaching when Christianity will be almost as openly disavowed in the language, as in fact it is already supposed to have disappeared from the conduct of men; when infidelity will be held to be the necessary appendage of a man of fashion, and to believe will be deemed the indication of a feeble mind. . . .

In whatever class or order of society Christianity prevails, she sets herself to counteract the particular mode of selfishness to which that class is liable. Affluence she teaches to be liberal and beneficent; authority to bear its faculties with meekness . . . [She also teaches] that the peace of mind which religion offers indiscriminately to all ranks affords more true satisfaction than all the expensive pleasures which are beyond the poor man's reach . . . and finally that all human distinctions will soon be done away, and the true followers of Christ will all, as children of the same Father, be alike admitted to the possession of the same heavenly inheritance.

A Practical View of Professed Christians Contrasted with Real Christianity (1797)

Questions

1. What difference did Wilberforce's calling make to his nation and the world? And if indeed Parliament was Wilberforce's parish, how did he do?

2. In his book *Halftime,* Bob Buford argues that as we move into the second half of our lives, from stressing success to a focus on significance, what we have learned will often be applicable to what we do after the halftime adjustments. How was this borne out in Wilberforce's life?

3. How was Wilberforce a model of prudence—that is, what actions should one take and when should they be taken? In this regard, how critical was the Clapham brotherhood to Wilberforce's achievements?

4. Wilberforce's love of reading reminds us of Blaise Pascal, one of the most thoughtful Christians of the seventeenth century, who divided the people he encountered into "those who strive with all their might to learn and those who live without troubling themselves or thinking about it." Ask yourself, "What have I read during the past month that truly nourished my mind?" If you're discouraged by your answer, agree with a friend that in the next month you'll read one book together and discuss it.

5. William Wilberforce seems to have taken the teaching of Jesus literally, that "in [Him] we can do all things" (Phil 4:13). Using Wilberforce as a model, what might you do in your own sphere of influence?

For further reading

Hague, William. *William Wilberforce: The Life of the Great Anti-Slave Trade Campaigner* Orlando: Harcourt, 2007.

Pollock, John. *Wilberforce.* New York: St. Martin's, 1977.

Pura, Murray Andrew. *Vital Christianity: The Life and Spirituality of William Wilberforce.* Toronto: Clements, 2002.

Wilberforce, William. *A Practical View of the Prevailing Religious System of Professed Christians in the Higher and Middle Classes of this Country Contrasted with Real Christianity.* Peabody, MA.: Hendrickson, 2006. Online: http://www.gutenberg.org/files/25709/25709-h/25709-h.htm.

CHAPTER 5

Oswald and Biddy Chambers

He is preparing us for what He is preparing for us.
Oswald Chambers, aged 34

Story: Can calling change?

In a cemetery in Cairo, Egypt is a gravestone which reads, "A believer in Jesus Christ." Below it is an image of a Bible opened to Luke 11:13—a text decisive in one man's life. Oswald Chambers had told his friends: "I feel I shall be buried for a time, hidden away in obscurity; then suddenly I shall flame out, do my work, and be gone."[1] After he died was his work done? Can callings change in unforeseen ways and, somehow, continue even after our lives end?

Soon after I became a believer I was given a copy of *My Utmost for His Highest*, a daily devotional that has the name Oswald Chambers underneath the title. I've been reading it now for over four decades. In this I'm hardly alone: two generations after the book was first published readers across the globe begin their day studying words spoken by Oswald Chambers because someone else's calling led her to transcribe them, and years later organize them into books.

It is 2459 miles between Cairo and Aberdeen, Scotland, where in 1874 Oswald Chambers was born, the fourth son of a Baptist minister recalled

1. B. Chambers, *Oswald Chambers*, 33.

by his granddaughter as a dour Scot, "a very, very hard, hard man."[2] Oswald Chambers spent his boyhood years in nearby Perth, showing few signs of that intense devotion to the life of the mind that would characterize his adulthood. Rather, his passion was for art. When he was fifteen, the Chambers moved to London. Because of his passion for music and art, and because he did them well and thus sensed they were given him by God, Chambers sought out a career that would encompass his gifts. His practical-minded father had him apprenticed to an engraver, perhaps a reflection of the senior Chambers's sense of his son's emerging artistic talents. But after getting off a streetcar on his way to work, Chambers injured himself so severely that the apprenticeship ended.

Following his accident the young Chambers clashed with his father over Reverend Chambers's moral objections to his son entering art school. To Oswald the arts were from God: "Music, Poetry, Art, through which God breathes/His Spirit of Peace into the Soul."[3] Eventually winning over his father, Chambers entered what is now the prestigious Royal College of Art. Finishing his degree at age eighteen, he then struggled both to earn a living and to discern God's will for what he understood to be his calling, to redeem the art world. Chambers wrote a long letter to Chrissie Brain, his closest female friend, worth considering at length because it reveals so clearly his then sense of purpose and the means to achieve it:

> "Whom shall I send to proclaim the salvation of the aesthetic kingdom, who will go for us?" Then through all my weakness, my sinfulness and my frailty my soul cried, "Here am I, send me." I would as soon drown myself as undertake such a work unless He was with me, unless He called me, unless He sent me.

Chambers understood he couldn't do the work were he not called to it, hence the echo of Isaiah. He then turned to contemplating the work he assumed he was being prepared for.

> [T]here is something wrong somewhere, else Christians and art, music and poetry would not in their training be so opposed to Christ, mark you. It is the training that is wrong, not the visible works of music and art and poetry. Again I say, I do not know how this is to be accomplished, but if God calls, God will guide and I know that this kingdom shall become the kingdom of His Son. . . . [F]or Jesus sake, I plunge into arduous hard study to prepare me,

2. Chambers Papers, Box 10, Folder 23.
3. Chambers, *Insane.*

that men must listen, because of the double authority which I must have—of the knowledge and of God.

Chambers was fully convinced concerning the integration of all spheres of culture creation—hence his "double authority." After discerning his vocation he went on sounding like Elijah in the wilderness.

Our Saviour, as far as my limited knowledge goes, has no representative to teach, to reprove, to exhort—and Oh Spirit of God, Thou knowest, an ambition, a longing, a love has seized me powerfully, and has convinced me of the lack. I know my life work is in . . . proving Christ's redemption for the aesthetic kingdom.

Chambers then finished this line of thought.

[T]here is a crying need . . . for a fearless writer . . . above pandering to popular taste, to warn and exhort that all the kingdoms of this world are to become Christ's—that artists, poets and musicians be good and fearless Christians.[4]

To achieve what he had discerned his life work to be, he returned to his beloved Scotland and entered the University of Edinburgh to study art. Intellectually fulfilled, the call, however, became less clear. "From my very childhood," he wrote while at Edinburgh, "the persuasion has been that of a work, strange and great, an experience deep and peculiar—it has haunted me ever and ever." While Chambers could recall, "It spoke clearly to me about my coming here and I came," now, however, there was doubt, producing the first of many spiritual crises he was to experience.[5]

Chambers waited until God spoke to him again, and in the meantime engaged in an intense study of philosophy, ethics, and poetry, as well as psychology—a new subject in the academic firmament—realizing another set of gifts to add to his collection. He struggled with the tension between his growing intellectual passion, which seemed to be of God, and his worsening financial straits, that the same God was reducing his prospects of success. Thus was Chambers vexed: God had equipped him, but had somehow forgotten to provide the means for the intended work. "I've reached the edge of human patience . . . and cry, 'How long, O Lord, how long.'"[6] Such despair—knowing what but not knowing how—is sometimes most rampant in the brightest person with the broadest range of interests.

4. B. Chambers, *Oswald Chambers*, 26–27; McCasland, *Oswald Chambers*, 41–42.

5. B. Chambers, *Oswald Chambers*, 29–30.

6. McCasland, *Oswald Chambers*, 54.

Out of this crisis came a new notion—that of becoming a minister. But this would mean turning *from* the call to study art, which had seemed so clearly suited to both his gifts and passion, *to* something about which he harbored serious doubts. He couldn't see how the new notion could be combined with his passion for art—which would in his mind be the point. Regarding clergy,

> the majority know not the love of beauty as an artist knows it, and artists as a rule will not heed ministers. The duty of ministers is to instruct the people out of the bigoted notions against art. It is for the man of God artist to enter this aesthetic kingdom and live and struggle and strain for its salvation and exaltation.[7]

Despondent, he reflected that, "everything I have tried has been hopelessly unsuccessful."[8]

Desperate, he hiked up to Arthur's Seat, in the hills above Edinburgh, to spend the night praying, and heard God speak to him—out loud: "I want you in My service—but I can do without you."[9] Ouch! When he returned to his room the next morning there was a letter from Dunoon Theological College, a school in a tiny Scottish town near Glasgow. This was catharsis, for the mysterious letter from Dunoon intensified Chambers's conviction about his new calling: "My whole being is ablaze and passionately on fire to preach Christ. All my art aims are swallowed up in this now."[10] This deepening sense of a new vocation expanded after he heard a talk by Hudson Taylor—the famous missionary to China—that the true meaning of "have faith in God" was "have faith in the faithfulness of God, not in your own faithfulness."[11] When the principal of Dunoon asked him to come to the college both as a student and as an art teacher, Chambers saw how he could combine earlier with more recent thinking about his vocation and, critically, resolve his money crisis. Thus would all his tensions—vocational, financial, spiritual—be resolved.

At age twenty-two he moved the eighty miles from Edinburgh to Dunoon, from a world-class university to an obscure school which consisted of thirty students. Friends and family thought the move senseless. Foolish or not, he stayed on for nine years and was to draw on that experience when

7. Chambers Papers, Box 10, Folder 23.

8. McCasland, *Oswald Chambers*, 58.

9. B. Chambers, *Oswald Chambers*, 16.

10. Lambert, *Oswald Chambers*, 31.

11. McCasland, *Oswald Chambers*, 59.

fifteen years later he opened a similar college in London. While at Dunoon he taught drawing in the local elementary school, developed a club to study Robert Browning (his favorite poet), performed as a classical musician and as a comedian, wrote short stories, mentored younger students, and lectured on philosophy at the college. This constellation of activities provides an important insight: God may not let us in on what's going on even while we desperately seek clarity, but he never wastes an experience to which he brings us.

Meanwhile, it is time to turn to the second character in this story. Gertrude Hobbs, born in suburban London, was the daughter of a bankrupt baker turned clerk. I'll refer to her as Biddy, because that's the nickname bestowed on her by Oswald Chambers. Biddy Hobbs spent much of her childhood suffering from bronchitis—which meant she missed much of her formal schooling. She left school for good in her early teens, and thereafter took a shorthand correspondence course, reaching the remarkable ability to take down more than 250 words per minute—near the maximum of what was physically possible. After her father died when she was fifteen, in order to help support her family she utilized her skills working as a secretary, first for a general and later for a lawyer. Recall, God never wastes our experiences, or as the Chambers's daughter Kathleen recalled regarding this context, "My father always used to talk about God's order in the haphazard."[12]

In 1905, aged twenty-two, Biddy met Oswald Chambers when he was a guest in the church his brother Arthur served as the pastor and where the Hobbs were members. Three years later Hobbs left Britain with a friend to explore secretarial jobs in New York City. Oswald Chambers was also on board the ship, on his way to minister in America.

Conversion

How and when Biddy Hobbs become a believer remains unclear—even her daughter was unaware of the details. But if her experience in coming to faith may have been relatively straightforward, the same could not be said for Oswald Chambers.

---

12. Chambers Papers, Box 10, Folder 23; B. Chambers, *Oswald Chambers*, 291, 306, 313, 314.

When he was sixteen Oswald Chambers was, to use his words, "born again as a lad."[13] But from that moment on he struggled with keeping part of himself from God, and with a strong sense of his hypocrisy. Now twenty-two and teaching philosophy at Dunoon College, moved by having heard a talk, he went to his room and prayed for the baptism of the Holy Spirit, not entirely certain what that meant.

What in fact it meant was a very dark night of the soul, lasting four years. With each offering up to God the things he loved, including the woman he thought he would marry, his inner emptiness only increased. The words from a poem Chambers composed at the time reveal the inner life of a profoundly troubled man: "dark moods of the mind . . . the soul must bleed."[14] Another comment is equally telling, from a church at which he had preached: "Dinna send us yon long-haired swearin' parson."[15] Internal angst led to hellfire sermons—which, apparently, were not very compelling.

Believers doubt and despair, and Chambers did both. He recalled years later: "I knew that if what I had was all the Christianity there was, the thing was a fraud." For Chambers one biblical promise turned things around: "Then Luke xi. 13 got hold of me—'If ye then, being evil, know how to give good gifts to your children, how much more shall your Heavenly Father give the Holy Spirit to them that ask Him?'"[16] He still wavered: how could someone as depraved as he believed himself to be ask God for such a gift? Yet, Jesus said claim the gift and then testify to having done so.

Desperate, Chambers attended a meeting in Dunoon town sponsored by the League of Prayer, an organization we'll encounter again in the story that follows. The woman in charge asked those present to pray, but prior to that sang, "Touch me again, Lord." Chambers recalled that moment: "I felt nothing, but I knew emphatically my time had come, and I rose to my feet. I had no vision of God, only a sheer dogged determination to take God at His Word and to prove this thing for myself, and I stood up and said that."[17] He had been baptized by the Holy Spirit, but like Chambers we only realize such things fully by looking backward.

13. Chambers, "How the Blessing Came," 4.

14. Chambers, *Afterward*.

15. B. Chambers, *Oswald Chambers*, 38.

16. Chambers, "How the Blessing Came," 4.

17. Ibid.

While he now had peace Chambers remained spiritually empty, asking the principal of the college what was going on. The principal—who had long been his spiritual mentor—informed him that Chambers had received what he had claimed. Chambers realized that he wanted the power only so that he would be praised by those who witnessed the impact of his preaching—not unlike Simon the magician in Acts 8. What had been empty was now filled—with love of God rather than self-love. At that moment Oswald Chambers was born again—again; the Holy Spirit had spoken to him, which in turn triggered development of a new calling.

Chambers had written dozens of poems between 1892 and 1901. The last before his moment of renewal, dated September 30, 1901, ends with these lines:

> O do hear me, O do hear me,
> Else I think my heart will break;
> In its longing, be Thou near me,
> And my burning thirst—oh slake!
>
> O Lord Jesus, hear my crying
> For a consecrated life,
> For I bite the dust in trying
> For release from this dark strife.[18]

During the remainder of his life he composed only two more poems, within a few days of each other four years later, and then a year after that wrote, looking back to the impact of his baptism of the Holy Spirit five years previously of the joy and peace that replaced his dark strife. Chambers concluded that he would now live in light of the poetry that had been so deeply embedded in his sense of being. From age twenty-seven on to the end of his life he would be free. God had spent a decade forging him into a man free from self, free to hear—deeply—God call him.

Thereafter the life of Oswald Chambers was characterized by a deep desire to abandon everything for the sake of God, and to encourage others to do the same. He wrote later, clearly autobiographically:

> A sanctified soul may be an artist, or a musician; but he is not a sanctified artist or musician: he is one who expresses the message of God through a particular medium. As long as the artist or musician imagines he can consecrate his artistic gifts to God, he is deluded. Abandonment of ourselves is the kernel of consecration,

18. McCasland, *Oswald Chambers*, 315.

not presenting our gifts, but presenting ourselves without reserve
to Christ.[19]

Chambers termed the baptism of the Holy Spirit a new beginning rather than an arrival. He explained it in 1908 to a friend: "You ask a question about the baptism of the Holy Ghost—did I get there all at once, or easily? No, I did not. Pride and the possession of the high esteem of my many Christian friends kept me out for long enough."[20] This is the problem with letting friends—and even family—tell us what we should do with our lives. Chambers went on: "But immediately I was willing to sacrifice all and put myself on the Altar, which is Jesus Himself, [and] all was begun and done." He needed to focus not on doing but being. In effect, at age twenty-seven, having experienced years of "deeper pain than reason could stand,"[21] Chambers had abandoned himself to God and begun to live out his new calling.

Calling

Rather like Hannah More, God called Chambers *from* focusing on his gifts in art, poetry, music, and philosophy (which Chambers hoped would provide a livelihood), *to* a vocation that would employ those gifts but in his case never provide a secure income, quite unlike More's situation. The comparison reveals there is not one pattern among believers and based on the two Chambers, not one trajectory within a single believer's life.

Thus far we have seen Oswald Chambers's sense of calling change from artist to teaching art and philosophy to preparing to teach a Christianity unafraid of the life of the mind. His brother Arthur had visited Wales to investigate the spectacular revival that began there in 1904, and he piqued Oswald's interest in global evangelism. As a consequence, he left Dunoon in 1905 to pursue a career as an itinerant minister, having been ordained "to the work of the ministry" rather than by a denomination.[22] He was without consistent financial support, simply acting on his calling. His niece Irene recalled his communication style: "He always spoke in the same natural way; clear, colloquial, trenchant words in his rather penetrating voice with its Scottish tang. He used no poetic word-spinning and no emotional ap-

19. Lambert, *Oswald Chambers*, 38.

20. B. Chambers, *Oswald Chambers*, 122.

21. Ibid., 123.

22. *Dunoon Herald*, May 12, 1899.

peal, for he had no time for intellectual or spiritual bluff."[23] But lest the reader think this is the end of the story, Oswald and Biddy's callings were nowhere near finished.

Having met Juji Nakada, a Japanese evangelist, Chambers determined to go into all the world. And so in 1906 he began a four-year teaching tour associated with the League of Prayer, having "never felt God's call so clear, or His meaning so certain."[24] At the very beginning of his travels he reflected on how his past played into his future: "I am growing more and more grateful for the tremendous, and as I once thought, unnecessary schooling I gave myself in philosophy and psychology in my Edinburgh and Dunoon days; I see now that the mental discipline is invaluable for God's work."[25]

The League of Prayer had been founded in 1891 by Richard Reader Harris, a London lawyer and lay Methodist minister, as a nondenominational fellowship focused on reviving the church. Like the Salvation Army, the League was an outcome of the late nineteenth-century Wesleyan-holiness movement. It emphasized experiencing the power of the Holy Spirit sometime after a believer's initial salvation, so as to engender a deeper faith. Women were encouraged to engage in ministry, and later on one of the League's regular speakers was Biddy Chambers. While remaining a Baptist, Oswald was happy to partner with Harris but as well Nakada, first in Britain, then in the United States, and finally in Japan. Time and again he was adventurous, even silly, holding to a line he suggested to Biddy: "Keep carefully careless about everything but your relationship to him"; a student years later recalled him as "the most irreverent Reverend I had ever met!"[26] When in the United States his heart was warmed when he experienced black believers in a church setting for the first time. "They laugh and shout 'Glory,' and interrupt the preacher to tell the audience an incident they think illustrates the point—gloriously unconventional."[27]

On board the ship on which Chambers and Nakada sailed from Seattle to Japan was another passenger, a brilliant unbelieving Yale graduate ten years Chambers's junior. The more he spoke with Chambers the more amazed he was, characterizing him as a "musician of no mean education" who as well was painting thought-provoking pictures. Chambers noted

23. B. Chambers, *Oswald Chambers*, 45.

24. Ibid., 55, 58, 118.

25. Ibid., 61.

26. Chambers Papers, Box 8, Folder 9; B. Chambers, *Oswald Chambers*, 154.

27. B. Chambers, *Oswald Chambers*, 56.

in his diary that the two spoke on art, philosophy, religion, and psychology, the young man concluding that Chambers was a remarkable man.[28] Their conversations revealed that if evangelism and revival was one side of Chambers's calling, integration of the life of the mind with the life of faith was the other. Spiritual renewal led Chambers to expand his reading list, which included not just orthodox theologians but the novels of Honoré de Balzac and the plays of Henrik Ibsen. Though contemporary conservative believers considered the works of the last particularly scandalous, Chambers found such writings gave him important insights into the human condition, even if those perceptions, lacking a biblical dimension, were unable to comprehend the complexity of the human heart. What such a rigorous approach made possible was to think about the world from intersecting spiritual and intellectual perspectives.

Chambers read anything he could get his hands on, and in writings as well as his life we see the Holy Spirit and his mind powerfully engaged. "My books! I cannot tell you what they are to me—silent, wealthy, loyal lovers. To look at them, to handle them, and to re-read them! I do thank God for my books with every fibre of my being."[29] His copy of Plato was, in the words of his daughter, "absolutely crammed full of notes."[30] Chambers is then *the* model for the modern believer. Those of us who emphasize "just believe" ought to heed his challenge to cultivate our minds; those of us who privilege thinking at the expense of the emotional life need to spend some time introducing the left side of our brain to its ally, the right side.

Chambers's pet peeve was intellectual slovenliness disguised as spirituality. To John Skidmore, a burned out colleague who when asked what he read replied, "nothing but the Bible and books directly associated with it," Chambers responded, "The trouble is you have allowed part of your brain to stagnate for want of use." He wrote out a list of fifty books dealing with contemporary thought, and followed this up with a letter urging his friend

> to *soak, soak, soak* in philosophy and psychology, until you know more of these subjects than ever you need consciously to think. It is ignorance of these subjects on the part of ministers and workers that has brought our evangelical theology to such a sorry plight

---

28. Stark, *Letters*, 6–7; B. Chambers, *Oswald Chambers*, 76.

29. B. Chambers, *Oswald Chambers*, 65–66.

30. Chambers Papers, Box 10, Folder 23.

... The man who reads only the Bible does not, as a rule, know it or human life.[31]

Chambers has this message for us today: The minds of believers need to be applied to the texts of our times.

Chambers understood the power of his own advice. During a week-long mission in Manchester in 1909, he had sought to win converts who would engage their minds in tackling the problems of hurting people in the real world; since his teens he had worked among the disadvantaged, including ex-convicts.[32] To this end he addressed the topic, "Christianity versus Socialism." The context might be understood from a subsequent writing: "If we are devoted to the cause of humanity, we shall soon be crushed and broken-hearted, for we shall often meet with more ingratitude from men than we would from a dog; but if our motive is love to God, no ingratitude can hinder us from serving our fellow men."[33] Integrate heart and mind or fail at calling; abide with God while nurturing your thought life.

Chambers wrote Biddy Hobbs, now his fiancée, that, "This mission has without question been the most wonderful and blessed of my life. What impressed me most was the way God opened up His word and poured out His Spirit. Years of study along the lines of philosophy and psychology and ethics suddenly seem to have come to fruition."[34] Now we might understand, as Chambers put it: "God never gives us anything accidental."[35]

In the years after 1908 when Chambers and Biddy Hobbs had renewed their acquaintance on the ship, he to launch his world tour, she to have a spell of secretarying in America, the two discovered that they shared a deep love for art, music, nature, animals, and reading books. They began a correspondence that continued after they separately returned to Britain. Following an eighteen-month engagement they married in 1910. He had written her during the engagement: "I have no home to offer you. I have no money to give you. I have the great wild world and His commission—Go and make disciples." In the following months a shared calling emerged in his mind, that God was "preparing us both for the same power and service."[36] They

31. B. Chambers, *Oswald Chambers*, 94–95.

32. Ibid., 15, 23.

33. Chambers, *Utmost for His Highest*, February 23.

34. Chambers Papers, Box 17, Folder 5.

35. *Utmost for His Highest*, April 27.

36. Chambers Papers, Box 17, Folder 5.

were soon to discover—twice over—that theirs was to be a complementary calling.

Achievements

Prior to World War I the League of Prayer wanted to establish a training center whose focus would be teaching the Bible and training in holiness. Both Chambers came to believe that it was God's will for them to accomplish this by launching a college in London, and also to begin publishing some of Oswald's lectures. "I want *us* to write and preach," Oswald put it to Biddy in 1909; "if I could talk to you and you shorthand it down and then type it, what ground we could get over!"[37]

The League leased a building on Clapham Common, the London neighborhood associated with both Hannah More and William Wilberforce. Chambers served as principal and lecturer at the Bible Training College; Biddy served as the "Lady Superintendent," taught, practiced hospitality, and transcribed almost every lecture her husband gave. She had previously taken shorthand notes on what Oswald said in his speaking engagements, years later telling their daughter that it allowed her to listen better. Thus it was that the two Chambers moved away from preaching to teaching, and from evangelism to equipping young people to seek first God's kingdom and righteousness, from a peripatetic to a settled life. Biblical Psychology became a core class at the Bible Training College and the first book that bore the name of Oswald Chambers.

When the college opened in January 1911 it had no students; and then the first one left after one day. Most of us would have been overwhelmed by a feeling of failure. The response of Chambers was to teach courses across London. In time the college had twenty-five full-time residential students—half men and half women—who were joined by fifty day students, hundreds of other part-timers and still others who took courses by correspondence. One student recalled that the college, which was also the Chambers's home, "kept open house for the broken, the bruised, the unfortunate, for the old, the forlorn, and the weary."[38] Students came from a variety of denominations and social backgrounds: one was a Trinity College, Dublin professor, another a seamstress. Earlier in his life Chambers had been obsessed about having sufficient money to pursue his vocation. Never financially secure,

37. Chambers Papers, Box 17, Folder 5.
38. Ashe, *Book of the College*, 16.

he continued to teach at other locations in London. But Chambers had learned that being without money meant having to live by faith. Thus he turned down an offer of endowment, and the college consistently had just enough financial resources to survive.

Chambers saw the school's purpose to equip—spiritually, intellectually, and as a community—a cohort of students for whatever ministry God called them to, to put them "into a right spiritual atmosphere" to discern the will of God for their lives, to introduce them to God so that they would let Him guide them:

> One student a year who hears God's call would be sufficient for God to have called the Bible Training College into existence. This college has no value as an organization, not even academically. Its sole value for existence is for God to help Himself to lives.[39]

The class on biblical ethics Chambers taught reflected his commitment to training students to think for themselves—and to think hard. Sarah Mayhew noted a challenge by Oswald in 1913 from a lecture entitled, "Look Again and Think": "There is so little thinking done—thinking about what God has said we are to think about in His Book. If we had fewer spiritual ambitions & enterprises & more thinking we should make fewer mistakes about things and know God as he is."[40] His lectures were designed to engage minds, so that as a teacher his challenge for students was to take their learning seriously.

When students recalled their years at the college it was often, as in the words of Beatrice Lilley, "for the teaching and help received from His servants the Rev. and Mrs. Chambers."[41] One student remembered the school as "a place of strenuous peace, a sane and wholesome house of life, where for each student, heart and mind and bodily powers of intellect and will are kept at full stretch," another recalling "the terrifically high standard put before us."[42] Each day began with prayer at 8 a.m., continued with lectures from morning through evening and ended with prayer at 10 p.m.; every week there were written exams. The deep experience of committed community touched scores of students.

---

39. McCasland, *Oswald Chambers*, 195; Chambers Papers, Box 4, Folder 14, Box 10, Folder 23; Chambers, *Utmost for His Highest*, November 3.

40. Chambers Papers, Box 4, Folder 14.

41. Ibid.

42. Ibid.; B. Chambers, *Oswald Chambers*, 148.

In 1913 Oswald wrote his wife that, "I never see my way. I know God who guides so I fear nothing. I have never far-seeing plans, only confident trust."[43] In this he anticipated what was to follow. The Bible Training College remained open through the first year of World War I. By that point the institution had trained 106 men and women—forty of them becoming missionaries. When war broke out in 1914, Chambers wrote in the magazine of the League of Prayer: "War is a conflict of wills either in individuals or in nations, and just now there is a terrific conflict of wills in nations." He went on to reveal an understanding shared by very few of his contemporaries: "War, such as the history of the world has never known, has now begun," but encouraged his readers not to be worried and to trust God.[44]

As the war went on Chambers experienced "a vague desolation" in what he knew to be "the desperate spiritual need of our soldiers."[45] That is, he heard a new calling—combining teaching with a ministry of encouragement. The seeds were sown late in 1914, when he wrote in his prayer journal: "The wonder has begun to stir in me—is this [the Bible Training College] Thy place for me."[46] A number of the school's graduates were already serving as chaplains. By spring 1915 Chambers had decided to work with the British army; in June he announced the College was to close temporarily, as "in obedience to God's call" he had volunteered.[47] His Bible reading had repeatedly pointed him to this new venture, and subsequently Chambers requested the YMCA designate him as a military chaplain. Oswald and Biddy ended the courses at the Bible Training College at the close of the school year, intending to restart them when peace was restored.

In October 1915 Oswald Chambers left Britain to serve British, Australian, and New Zealand troops who began arriving ten months earlier to join the Mediterranean Expeditionary Force in Egypt, in effect relocating the Bible Training College from Clapham to Cairo. Biddy and their two and-one-half-year-old daughter Kathleen followed two months later, joining Chambers, who had been posted to Zeitoun, a camp then six miles outside Cairo. Although in existence since the war began, in early 1916 the Imperial School of Instruction was established there for training in

43. Lambert, *Oswald Chambers*, 41–42.

44. *Tongues of Fire*, September 1914.

45. *Tongues of Fire*, August 1915; Chambers Papers, Box 4, Folder 14.

46. McCasland, *Oswald Chambers*, 196.

47. Ashe, *Book of the College*, 18.

advanced warfare techniques. The YMCA then constructed its compound adjacent to the camp.

Chambers had possibly been drawn to the locale by stories circulating in Britain of "Oriental vice" among troops in Egypt.[48] But he never discussed the negative—that the job of a chaplain was to get the immorality out of the men by distracting them—but rather the positive: to get the spiritual life in. As he put it to Biddy in 1916, "Remember we stand for God, not goody-goodness."[49] An Australian might have put it to Oswald, Don't be a *wowser* (killjoy), mate; Oswald would have agreed with him: "Our bit is not the other fellow's bit."[50]

Having made the choice to move from the safety of London to a war zone, in one sense Chambers was part of a larger development. The number of British Army, denominational, and interdenominational chaplains rose from a few hundred to thousands during the course of the war. After a year, however, many became disillusioned and returned home. Chambers, in contrast, deepened his commitment to the soldiers he served, whose "eager thirst for Bible knowledge exceeds anything I have ever known."[51] He wrote one of his brothers that "what is required [here] is your best theology, your best philosophy and your best spirituality all the time."[52]

Across the battle zones of the First World War the YMCA built 10,000 huts to serve as venues for patriotic lectures and classes.[53] A photograph of the one in Zeitoun reveals a primitive lecture hall with an area set aside with desks for writing letters home. Chambers continued to develop the Zeitoun complex, adding a free Sunday tea, building new huts for his Bible classes, entertainment, and study, and a canteen with tables covered with white tablecloths and vases of flowers. He went beyond the standard YMCA "hut culture" in other ways, taking down disapproving notices and replacing them with humorous ones: "Beware! There is a religious talk here each evening!"[54] Ever the creative artist, on one occasion he staged a combined

---

48. *Service with Fighting Men*, i., 72; ii., 411; Barrett and Deane, *Australian Medical Corps in Egypt*, 65, 126; Elgood, *Egypt and the Army*, 251–52, 257.

49. Laugesen, *Australian Soldiers in the Great War*, 22–23; Chambers Papers, Box 8, Folder 9.

50. Thornton, *With the ANZACS in Cairo*, 109; Chambers Papers, Box 23, Folder 4.

51. B. Chambers, *Oswald Chambers*, 226.

52. Chambers Papers, Box 10, Folder 13.

53. Snape, *Back Parts of War*, 59–60, 63.

54. B. Chambers, *Oswald Chambers*, 280.

concert and boxing match for 1200 troops. "It is just these sordid actualities that make the right arena for Our Lord's Reality," Chambers noted in his diary. "I am devoted to the plain rough human stuff as it is, and it is glorious to know that the reality of God's presence is but increased by things as they actually are."[55] In this he caught the mood of soldiers who rebelled against the British army trying to "order cheerfulness."[56]

In this photograph, taken in the autumn of 1916, Chambers stands by a fifteen-foot tall sign near the study hut he had built for his classes—which he termed the new Bible Training College. Beginning in 1916 YMCA chaplains wore military-style clothing, and by dressing in a khaki uniform Chambers identified with the soldiers. As the sign advertised, he did intellectually as well: "I shall take subjects along the lines of Religious problems raised by the war and invite questions."[57] He used the same pedagogy in Egypt as he had in London, hence the term, "blackboard lecture" (featuring an extensive outline so listeners could follow complicated concepts). For his part Oswald thought that "The soldiers form the keenest set of students I have ever had."[58] He took spiritual crises head on, engaging soldiers who had or were about to face death. On one occasion Chambers noted that "These men go to Gallipoli on Monday and certainly half will never return, and they know it."[59] His point was to offer life.

Oswald Chambers
Wheaton College (Illinois), Oswald Chambers Papers, SC-122

William Jessop, the American YMCA director in Egypt, remembered Chambers "as a man of remarkable mind" whose unique approach to teaching appealed both to believers and doubters.[60] Chambers talked about what troubled the men, Jessop recalled, treating their concerns from a biblical

55. Ibid., 215.

56. Woodfin, *Camp and Combat*, 81.

57. B. Chambers, *Oswald Chambers*, 264.

58. *Tongues of Fire*, March 1916.

59. B. Chambers, *Oswald Chambers*, 214.

60. Chambers Papers, Box 8, Folder 9; B. Chambers, *Oswald Chambers*, 251.

standpoint; "every evening you will find in his class fifty interested soldiers, men who take notice, study and think."[61]

What Oswald and Biddy Chambers offered these young soldiers was human kindness in the form of food, conversation, stimulating lectures, and prayer. Meals were available to all, who were then invited to come back if they wished for the evening lecture—sometimes taught by Biddy. As well as the blackboard lectures five evenings per week there were up to four different services on Sunday, and counseling—which was to be one of Biddy's future callings. The Chambers touched the lives of perhaps tens of thousands of men—and not just those who wandered into the Zeitoun hut. Oswald traveled to other locations, giving talks and providing encouragement, including at a hospital housing men with venereal diseases. Thus while one contemporary, praising the work of the YMCA, argued that, "out there . . . men stand most in need not of preaching, but of service,"[62] the Chambers, understanding the complexity of the human heart, understood they needed both—together.

Soldiers' clubs with their leisure activities to counter boredom was the standard YMCA approach.[63] The Chambers offered more, and the men responded by showing up in increasing numbers. "These classes are a contradiction to the general idea that men will not come to religious talks," Chambers observed in November 1916. "[C]ertainly my blackboard outline offered no attraction to anyone not a thinking man!"[64] Biddy told their daughter that Oswald "used to very often finish the talk at the devotional hut in the evening by saying to all these men, 'Whether you agree with what I've said is a matter of moonshine as long as you begin to think.'"[65] After experiencing the Chambers' lectures some of the soldiers planned to attend the Bible Training College after the war.

Biddy not only gave lectures and sermons but her hospitality, first perfected at the college in London, was legendary: "The letters she has received from mothers and wives and sisters and fathers and brothers," Oswald noted, "are in themselves a deep testimony to a most unconscious ministry of wife and mother and woman."[66] Their joint work in Egypt was but another

61. Chambers Papers, Box 8, Folder 12.

62. Whitehair, *Out There*, 70.

63. *Service with Fighting Men*, ii., 411–12.

64. B. Chambers, *Oswald Chambers*, 270.

65. Chambers Papers, Box 10, Folder 23.

66. McCasland, *Oswald Chambers*, 251.

chapter in their life together, recalled simply by their daughter: "They both of them loved people."[67]

Countless soldiers became believers through the Chambers' teaching and by observing their dedication to them. "Do you think God will hear me if I pray?" one soldier asked Oswald in December 1915. Chambers quoted Luke 11:13 to him, and that night wrote in his diary, "He has been won purely by prayer, he's well educated and sarcastic, but he's won, thank God."[68] A month later the soldier, a former opera singer, was with Chambers touring hospitals in Cairo, performing and testifying to the changes in his life.

Their sense of a dual vocation deepened in Egypt. After giving a series of evening lectures on Job in spring 1917, the Chambers decided to publish them as *Baffled to Fight Better*, the title from a Browning poem. Oswald wrote to a friend in Britain that Biddy was shaping the text and later noted in his diary how helpful she was preparing the final version for the publisher.[69]

From his first days in Egypt Oswald expressed delight in the spectacular desert sunrises and sunsets—which drew him back to his passion for art. His reading of the Bengali poet Rabindranath Tagore's recently published *Stray Birds* helped Chambers process the individuality of each dawn.[70] Following a lecture titled "The Inspiration of Architecture" he was "delighted to find how easily all my old art studies and knowledge came back again, fresh and vivid."[71] In these his last days, Chambers recognized his calling had come full circle.

> Perhaps the plunging horror and conviction of sin in my early life not only disrupted my Art calling and all the tendencies of those years, but switched me off by a consequent swing of the pendulum away from external beauties of expression . . . The beauty of form, of expression, of colour, all the fleeting features of the immense external fields of life, are again delighting me marvelously.[72]

With others the Chambers dreamed of peace after war. Kathleen Chambers recalled that her parents, who spent considerable time counseling soldiers,

67. Chambers Papers, Box 10, Folder 23.

68. McCasland, *Oswald Chambers*, 218.

69. B. Chambers, *Oswald Chambers*, 317; McCasland, *Oswald Chambers*, 249.

70. B. Chambers, *Oswald Chambers*, 306.

71. Ibid., 252.

72. Ibid., 312.

envisioned "they would have a home with a big garden where people could come and be at ease and find God and be healed of all the things that distressed them and worried them."[73] But for now the war dominated their thinking. In the autumn of 1917 Chambers prepared himself to follow the British army in the anticipated push toward Jerusalem. "I received the welcome news yesterday that I must hold myself in readiness to go up the line soon now."[74] Did Chambers sense still another calling?

Oswald Chambers preached his last sermon on October 14, 1917, "Disabling Shadows on the Soul," based on Ecclesiastes 12:5. The chapter begins with, "Remember your creator." Then we reach verse five:

> when people are afraid of heights
> and of dangers in the streets;
> when the almond tree blossoms
> and the grasshopper drags itself along
> and desire no longer is stirred.
> Then people go to their eternal home
> and mourners go about the streets.

Solomon taught, as presumably Oswald articulated in his sermon, that young people should not wait until the end of their lives to enter into a relationship with their Creator. Three days later Chambers became ill, and on October 29 he had an emergency appendectomy in the Red Cross hospital in Cairo. Although he seemed to recover a blood clot developed in his lung, and he died on November 15. That day Biddy told her daughter Kathleen, "Your daddy's gone to be with Jesus." Kathleen responded that that was wonderful and asked her mother why she was crying. "That, to my knowledge, is the only time I ever saw my mother cry, ever," Kathleen recalled. "She never did. She was always so determined that God has never made a mistake."[75]

Had he? Why would a loving God allow this to happen to a man who had lived a life full of significance after having struggled so long to reach spiritual maturity, who then in just a dozen years profoundly touched the lives of so many people, in Britain, America, Japan, and Egypt, when he had decades of fruitful work ahead of him? The Chambers had been married for fewer than eight years; Biddy was only thirty-three when her husband died. Couldn't God have prevented the blood clot? Oswald Chambers's answer in

73. Chambers Papers, Box 10, Folder 23; B. Chambers, *Oswald Chambers*, 286.

74. B. Chambers, *Oswald Chambers*, 324.

75. Chambers Papers, Box 10, Folder 23.

such situations was, "The astute mind behind the saint's life is the mind of God, not his own mind."[76] In ways I'm not sure I fully understand Chambers had done enough.

Tragic though his death was, 1917 was not the end of the story; far from it. Biddy Chambers, heartbroken, stayed on to serve the troops because the ministry had been *their* calling. At the same time she began transforming her husband's words into pamphlets, which the YMCA published and distributed. The pamphlets elicited positive responses, including one from a woman who wrote that she had been waiting for years to be able to read what Oswald Chambers had spoken. This led Biddy to tell her parents that, "It confirms me so much in the assurance I have that I am to go on getting everything I can printed. . . . We'll know someday all it has meant in people's lives." She added, "I am more and more grateful to have the work to do," later telling her daughter that God had given her the vocation of producing the publications.[77]

As well as the pamphlets she began producing books, assembling *The Shadow of an Agony* in summer 1918. "I find how much benefit I have got still from my old legal days, I mean getting into the habit of perfecting a thing by typing and retyping, and I am glad to have had all the experience of those other days." The work, she went on to suggest, remained theirs: "more and more I do feel that he is still part of it. . . . And just as one knows the presence of God so I growingly realise Oswald's presence, and so continually some word of his own comes with all the power and bracing that it ever did when he spoke."[78] When leafing through Oswald's Bible after his death Biddy found a draft letter her husband planned to send to his former students, ending with this thought: "Our main idea should be to remain where our business or calling or location finds us, allowing God to shape our circumstances as He providentially may."[79] Biddy had been doing precisely that.

In July 1919 Biddy and six-year old Kathleen returned to Britain. Penniless, for several years mother and daughter lived in a tiny cottage without electricity or running water. They later moved to Oxford and kept a boarding house for university students. Kathleen never recalled her mother being desperate, although she had to work very hard. "She would tell God we

---

76. Chambers, "With God at the Front," 1041.

77. McCasland, *Oswald Chambers*, 267; Chambers Papers, Box 10, Folder 23.

78. Chambers Papers, Box 17, Folder 1.

79. McCasland, *Oswald Chambers*, 266.

didn't have any money," Kathleen recollected. "She wasn't worried but she wanted Him to know that she trusted Him to give us, somehow for the money to come. And the money always came."[80] Their outlook is evident in a photograph taken after their arrival back in Britain. Biddy looks more determined than desperate, as does Kathleen, as if to say they had developed the strength to endure from outside in and then inside out.

Biddy and Kathleen Chambers
Wheaton College (Illinois), Oswald Chambers Papers, SC-122

Biddy became a lay Methodist preacher, riding her bicycle to teach in the countryside outside Oxford. Still dealing with a mountain of notes, in the basement of her Oxford boarding house she set up a study, typing each morning and again in the afternoon. From her record of Oswald's lectures and sermons Biddy composed *My Utmost for His Highest*, which she was able to get published in 1927; her choice of title went back to a 1909 note to her from Oswald.[81] Once the book was in print people began coming to her for spiritual guidance. Again we realize that no experience in the believer's life is wasted.

During his lifetime Oswald Chambers published just three books: *Biblical Psychology* (1912), *Studies in the Sermon on the Mount* (1915), and *Baffled to Fight Better* (1917). However, thanks to Biddy Chambers learning shorthand, taking down what he had spoken in lectures and classes, after a half-century of dedicated work compiling, organizing, entitling, and publishing her husband's words, more than fifty titles bear his name. Kathleen remembered her mother telling her that Oswald's deep knowledge of God produced delight in living, and that one life given over to God could change history.[82] Biddy's was one of those lives. Her name does not appear on any of the books but without four decades of work the world would never have known what Oswald said. Biddy died in 1966, Kathleen in 1997.

My Utmost for His Highest remains one of the highest selling religious books of all times. Through it far more people, perhaps millions, know the mind of Oswald Chambers than ever did when he was alive. This is the

80. Chambers Papers, Box 10, Folder 23.

81. Chambers Papers, Box 17, Folder 5.

82. Christian, *Searching*, 117; B. Chambers, *Oswald Chambers*, 12.

sense in which the calling of Oswald Chambers has never ceased; as one of his former students at the Bible Training College put it in the 1930s, thanks to the books, "we are still students of Oswald Chambers."[83] And so am I.

As we look back over both these two lives several themes emerge. One is that the Chambers held lightly to their own projects, always ready to let God guide them to something fresh. Thus they left four fruitful years at the college in London because men in the army during World War I needed what they could offer. And then in the last days of his life Oswald prepared himself to join the soldiers pushing into Palestine.

Second, the Chambers stand as models of integration of mind and spirit. In the early days of World War I Oswald understood, as did few others, how revolutionary the war was to be. Thus in July 1917 he wrote in his diary: "[A] scheme of socialistic propaganda is about to be enacted on a universal scale, with a mixture of astonishing good and atrocious bad, and until this has had its vogue Our Lord will not return, that is, if the past fairness to human schemes which God seems ever to have exhibited, is anything to go on."[84] This was less than four months before the Bolsheviks seized power in Russia, and he could not have known how the future would play out from any other source than the Holy Spirit. Biddy, according to her daughter, "could talk politically about anything" because she was so "widely read [and] interested in all sorts of aspects of everything."[85]

Finally, there was the vitality of Oswald Chambers's theology as heard by students and soldiers and thanks to Biddy available to us. Theology endures when it transcends project, creed, context, and religion by being focused on Jesus because, as Oswald Chambers put it, "theology is the thinking side of religion."[86] In one lecture at the Bible Training College in 1914 Chambers challenged students to ask whether their loyalty lay with Christ or their notion of him. In another he asked how believers were any different from other people. "To-day men are asking not so much—Is Christianity true; but is it real? Does it amount to anything in actual life?"[87] Those words might have been written last week rather than a century ago. Deep inner experience—holiness—and imagination applied to reflection

83. Chambers Papers, Box 4, Folder 14.

84. B. Chambers, *Oswald Chambers*, 311.

85. Chambers Papers, Box 10, Folder 23; Christian, *Searching*, 105–6.

86. B. Chambers, *Oswald Chambers*, 287.

87. Chambers, *Place of Help*, 1003.

on the Bible led him to engaging the world and current thought.[88] He taught that while the Holy Spirit was on offer for every believer it must be sought both intellectually and spiritually, to be acted on in one's life choices.[89] And this is what he had been doing—from Dunoon to Zeitoun.

Was he the greatest theologian of the twentieth century? It seems an absurd question, for he was not trained in the manner of what the academy understands as theology; nor did he teach—other than a few years at two tiny, obscure, and short-lived colleges. Yet listen to what his niece Irene recalled about him:

> The personal relationship of each individual soul to Jesus Christ was the essential of true living to him, and sects and Church membership and all the network of orthodox organized Christian life simply did not matter except as an individual choice. There was rarely, if ever, any of the negative side of religion about his teaching and nothing ever repressive or narrowing; discipline and self-denial must be self-imposed by God's guidance and not laid down by other people.[90]

He told audiences around the world: think for yourselves. On the way to Egypt in 1915 he wrote a sort of note to self in his diary: "It is such an inspiration to take human stuff as it actually is and drop the categorizing to which more or less we are all so liable, dealing with human beings as types. I do not believe in the type hunt. Every human being is his own type, therefore take him as a fact, not as an illustration of a prejudice."[91] What then is theology? Is it not helping humans realize with their hearts and minds and implement with their hands and feet how to be "mere believers" in the world? If so, then who has done this better for more people than Oswald Chambers—but only because of what Biddy accomplished with her husband's words.

When reading *Utmost for His Highest* Oswald Chambers seems remarkably self-assured about what he believed. The previous pages have revealed that this masks how he struggled to reach such a mature understanding of himself, his callings, and his Caller. He told Biddy in 1909, "It is always the meanest part of me that challenges my faith," countered by an entry in *Utmost for His Highest*: "I have never met a person I could despair

---

88. Randall, "Arresting People for Christ," 6.

89. Lambert, *Oswald Chambers*, 84–85, 89.

90. B. Chambers, *Oswald Chambers*, 45.

91. Ibid., 47.

of, or lose all hope for, after discerning what lies in me apart from the grace of God."[92] Reflecting on the last decade of his life it would seem the most loving part allowed his faith to flourish.

Epilogue

August 1968, half a century after Oswald and Biddy Chambers had departed Zeitoun saw the first of years of the appearance of the Virgin Mary at a church there, first to a Muslim bus mechanic, and eventually to Egyptian President Gamal Abdel Nasser. There were healings and other miracles associated with the appearances. In his first month at Zeitoun Oswald Chambers sensed the presence of angels, and several months later both he and an assistant had heard God declare, "It is I, be not afraid."[93] After his death a close family friend, Bessie Zwemer, told Biddy she had seen a radiant Oswald Chambers—and that he had spoken to her.[94] Biddy wrote to one of the Bible Training College students who had come to Egypt to work with the Chambers: "I do realize too his presence with us still in the spirit[;] we all do in this place which used to be so radiant with his life and his keen interest in every detail of it."[95] It could be that something of Oswald and Biddy Chambers remains in Egypt, in the biblical sense: "By faith Abel . . . still speaks, even though he is dead" (Heb 11:4).

92. Chambers Papers, Box 17, Folder 5; *Utmost for His Highest*, June 17.

93. B. Chambers, *Oswald Chambers*, 218, 225, 281.

94. McCasland, *Oswald Chambers*, 263–64.

95. Chambers Papers, Box 10, Folder 18.

His text

I am not saved by believing—I simply realize I am saved by believing. And it is not repentance that saves me—repentance is only the sign that I realize what God has done through Christ Jesus. The danger here is putting the emphasis on the effect, instead of on the cause. Is it my obedience, consecration, and dedication that make me right with God? It is never that! I am made right with God because, prior to all of that, Christ died. When I turn to God and by belief accept what God reveals, the miraculous atonement by the Cross of Christ instantly places me into a right relationship with God. And as a result of the supernatural miracle of God's grace I stand justified, not because I am sorry for my sin, or because I have repented, but because of what Jesus has done. The Spirit of God brings justification with a shattering, radiant light, and I know that I am saved, even though I don't know how it was accomplished.

The salvation that comes from God is not based on human logic, but on the sacrificial death of Jesus. We can be born again solely because of the atonement of our Lord. Sinful men and women can be changed into new creations, not through their repentance or their belief, but through the wonderful work of God in Christ Jesus which preceded all of our experience (see 2 Corinthians 5:17–19). The unconquerable safety of justification and sanctification is God Himself. We do not have to accomplish these things ourselves—they have been accomplished through the atonement of the Cross of Christ. The supernatural becomes natural to us through the miracle of God, and there is the realization of what Jesus Christ has already done—"*It is finished!*" (John 19:30).

My Utmost for His Highest, October 28

Her text

In the year that King Uzziah died, I saw the Lord—Isaiah 6:1.

Our soul's personal history with God is often an account of the death of our heroes. Over and over again God has to remove our friends to put Himself in their place, and that is when we falter, fail, and become discouraged. Let me think about this personally—when the person died who represented for me all that God was, did I give up on everything in life? Did I become ill or disheartened? Or did I do as Isaiah did and see the Lord?

My vision of God is dependent upon the condition of my character. My character determines whether or not truth can even be revealed to me. Before I can say, "I saw the Lord," there must be something in my character that conforms to the likeness of God. Until I am born again and really begin to see the kingdom of God, I only see from the perspective of my own biases. What I need is God's surgical procedure—His use of external circumstances to bring about internal purification.

Your priorities must be God first, God second, and God third, until your life is continually face to face with God and no one else is taken into account whatsoever. Your prayer will then be, "In all the world there is no one but You, dear God; there is no one but You."

Keep paying the price. Let God see that you are willing to live up to the vision.

My Utmost for His Highest, July 13, Biddy Chambers's birthday

Questions

1. How does the life of Oswald Chambers teach us that loving God with our minds is not a one-time act, but a process of day-to-day choices to obey God, applying our minds to the texts of our times?

2. There is a promise from the lives of the Chambers: "Faith is deliberate confidence in the character of God whose ways you may not understand at the time." As Oswald put it, "I never see my way. I know the God who guides so I fear nothing. I never have farseeing plans, only confident trust." In your experience, what does this look like?

3. Was the death of Oswald Chambers *untimely*? Do you agree with my contention that God wastes nothing? If so, how was this notion exemplified in lives of Oswald and Biddy Chambers? And have you wondered about your own dead ends?

4. How did Oswald and Biddy Chambers negotiate their major vocational transitions? Was this helpful history if you sense your need to do the same?

5. How many callings did Oswald Chambers have—or did he just one? How many callings did Biddy Chambers have—or did she just have one? Did they have a joint calling? If so, to what degree did this survive their deaths?

For further reading

Chambers, Oswald. *The Complete Works of Oswald Chambers*. Grand Rapids: Discovery House Publishers, 2000.

———. *My Utmost For His Highest*. London: Simpkin, Marshall & Co, 1927. Online: http://utmost.org/.

Christian, Martha [Marsha Drake]. *Searching for Mrs. Oswald Chambers*. Carol Stream: Tyndale House, 2008.

McCasland, David. *Oswald Chambers: Abandoned to God*. Grand Rapids: Discovery House 1993.

CHAPTER 6

G. K. Chesterton

Story: The Image of God—What Makes Us Matter

> Reason is from God,
> and when things are unreasonable
> there is something the matter.
> G. K. Chesterton, aged 53

AT OVER 300 POUNDS and standing six feet four inches tall, Gilbert Keith Chesterton's size matched his prodigious output: eighty books, hundreds of poems, several plays, 200 short stories, and 4,000 essays—each of them, regardless of subject, encapsulating their author's philosophy of life while disseminating some important idea. An enormous man, Chesterton never feared tackling large issues. Consideration of debates rooted in modern ways of thinking—modernism, as academics call it—led him to challenge the most important secular minds of his age. Firm in his belief that ortho-dox Christianity was the only antidote to the depredations of modernism, he sought to remind his contemporaries—and his works remind us—that there is a higher good than the current intellectual fad. That good is justice, the spiritual space between our self-interest and concern for others.

Among those on the receiving end of Chesterton's pen were the pro-moters of eugenics—whose purpose was to improve the human race by sterilization and selective breeding. *Eugenics* is a word that has disappeared from our vocabulary because of the horrors to which it led. But before there was a Nazi Germany eugenics, as with many modern notions, seemed an idea whose time had come. Chesterton countered arguments based on the best science and set forth by leading intellectuals by appealing to a historic understanding of human dignity. He put forward the rationale that our standing as persons was a gift, not a science project. As a starting point, the essential dignity of *all* human beings determined how we should regard each other. Therefore, humans should never be understood as objects to be manipulated—not by states, not by scientists, and not even by ourselves. The Incarnation affirmed what had been true from the beginning, that humans were created in the image of God.

Chesterton took what were at the time other unpopular stands—including opposition to his nation's imperialist aggression and questioning the moral basis of both capitalism and socialism. But he framed his arguments so winsomely that C. S. Lewis, who made his transition from atheism to Christianity by reading Chesterton, commented, "I did not need to accept what Chesterton said in order to enjoy it." By the time Lewis himself became a believer he claimed, "Chesterton had more sense than all the other moderns put together."[1]

To G. K. Chesterton, much of modern thinking was intellectually questionable and ethically dubious because of its twin weaknesses, a dogmatic skepticism about old things combined with "a hungry credulity about new things."[2] He critiqued modernism at its most dominant cultural moment by pushing its ideals to their logical ends in order to realize how they might shape the future. A good case was the secular myth of the progress of humanity, which was so lightly reasoned that it became vaguer as time went on, mutating into something like the modern cliché that the journey is more important than the destination. Chesterton saw this coming: "For it is a sin against reason to tell men that to travel hopefully is better than to arrive; and when once they believe it, they travel hopefully no longer."[3] As an alternative he offered the idea that to explore spiritually is to journey toward home; thoughtful nonbelievers realize this when they become aware of their homesickness.

Chesterton's worldview included a simple but significant sense of joy and wonder—of the huge scale of reality but as well his own garden; and gratitude—for creation, for friends, for his life, and for the historic church.

1. Lewis, *Surprised by Joy*, 190, 213.
2. Chesterton, *Autobiography*, 139.
3. Chesterton, *Outline of Sanity*, 236.

He once termed wonder "the basis of spirituality."[4] His contemporary Albert Einstein felt similarly: "He . . . who can no longer pause to wonder and stand rapt in awe, is as good as dead: his eyes are closed."[5] Chesterton was also deeply committed to the seemingly opposing concepts of free will and limits. He detested determinism, for it conveyed to humans they were automatons, while simultaneously putting before his readers metaphors such as frames, fences, boundaries, and edges, to draw the line somewhere in order to discern and even love what lies within. Both these notions challenged modern ideals—and in our time continue to do so. Many of us hold two contradictory principles, that our lives are constrained by great impersonal forces such as race, class, and gender, but that we should be free to do whatever we want.

A century ago Chesterton saw how modernism birthed such incoherence. Genuine liberty was for him not merely external but "something that works inwards."[6] Chesterton offers us the power to break free from the hold on our minds of such deterministic notions that poverty is destiny, while reading him helps free us from striving for the illusion of self-fashioned freedom. In his time, and now once again in ours, such striving finds it most exalted expression in discussions about manipulating the human body.

G. K. Chesterton was a fourth generation Londoner, the son of a less than ambitious realtor who with other men of his time believed "generally in new things, all the more because they were finding it increasingly difficult to believe in old things; and in some cases anything at all."[7] Educated at a prestigious private school, as a boy Chesterton imbibed what he later understood as "atheist orthodoxy,"[8] becoming, in his words, a pagan at twelve and a complete agnostic at sixteen. His outlook, expressed in several essays in his school's magazine, included the notion that Christianity stood for intolerance and bloodshed. Looking back he recalled that though "I was myself almost entirely Pagan and Pantheist," nonetheless "even during the period when I practically believed in nothing, I believed in what some have called 'the wish to believe.'"[9] A ravenous reader of the most cutting-edge thinkers, Chesterton's sense of wonder was at war with his brilliant intel-

4. Ker, *Chesterton*, 84.
5. Einstein, et al., *Living Philosophies*, 6.
6. Chesterton, *Autobiography*, 109.
7. Ibid., 33.
8. Ibid., 144.
9. Ibid., 145, 159.

lect. He was, one might say, homesick, reflected in the comment of one of his friends at the time: "We felt he was looking for God."[10]

Then in his late teens Chesterton experimented with the occult, finally stumbling upon Satan. "I am not proud in believing in the Devil," he later wrote. "I made his acquaintance by my own fault; and followed it up along lines which, had they been followed further, might have led me to devil-worship of the devil knows what."[11] This encounter with spiritual darkness came while Chesterton was studying art at the University of London, which he remembered as nightmarish, a time of personal depression—"plunging deeper and deeper as in a blind spiritual suicide"—and as "a period of drifting and doing nothing; in which I could not settle down to any regular work."[12] He doodled when listening to lectures and wrote when he should have been working on his art. Sloth is frequently a symptom of homesickness.

For a man who loved writing poetry, in his crisis Chesterton had no song. The more he read the less sense emerged from his era's unlimited optimism about achieving human perfectibility. As he was to maintain later in *The Everlasting Man* (1925), his was a post-Christian age; its members "still live in the shadow of the faith and have lost the light of the faith."[13] He may well have been excavating his own incoherent thinking of two decades earlier when he wrote that sentence. The means Chesterton used to work through his crisis are evident in *Orthodoxy* (1908): "A man is not really convinced of a philosophic theory when he finds that something proves it. He is only really convinced when he finds that everything proves it."[14] So it was that when he read the New Testament's Christ against what the books of the day preached about Jesus, he discovered the picture of a "business-like lion-tamer," a being "more strange and terrible than the Christ of the Church."[15]

To work out his thinking, Chesterton acted on the proposal of a friend that he drop art for journalism. Although in his autobiography Chesterton recalled, whimsically, that discovering his vocation was in the scheme of things unmerited—it was "outrageously unjust that a man should succeed

10. Ward, *Chesterton*, 26.

11. Chesterton, *Autobiography*, 85, 86.

12. Ibid., 96, 86.

13. Chesterton, *Everlasting Man*, 145.

14. Chesterton, *Orthodoxy*, 287.

15. Chesterton, *Everlasting Man*, 321, 325.

in becoming a journalist merely by failing to become an artist"[16]—his brother and others observed that when Chesterton was at art school he actually preferred to write. And so in his last year at the University of London he took up the study of history, politics, and languages, and for most of the rest of his life was a working journalist in one capacity or another.

Conversion

How do atheists become believers? In Chesterton's case he came to doubt his doubt, because the more he thought about the fashionable skepticism of his age the less sense it made. That is, he was part of the way home when he wrote at the time that "the world, clearly examined, does point with an extreme suggestiveness, to the existence of a spiritual world."[17] The more he thought deeply about his fellow human beings, the more he was drawn to believing the Christian story, for none other made as much sense.

Listening to speakers advocate the inevitably of progress, purposefully ignoring the bad alongside the good, he later recalled how troubling he took their arguments to be: "Even at that stage it occurred to me to ask, 'Supposing there is no difference between good and bad, or between false and true, what is the difference between up and down?'"[18] His "wish to believe" and the observation that it was usually clergymen who were able to articulate "some sort of test of some sort of truth" led him to the discovery that he was not an atheist.[19] This was the end of the beginning of his faith, but we need to go back to the beginning to understand why Chesterton reached that end.

"In the purely religious sense," Chesterton remembered, "I was brought up among people who were Unitarians and Universalists, but who were well aware that a great many people around them were becoming agnostics or even atheists."[20] The essential contradiction of modernist ideals was that having pulled up the roots of faith such as the historic creeds, half the modernist intellectuals argued that because God was in heaven all must be right with this world, while the other half doubted there was a God, and held that all was not right with the world. As a journalist Chesterton was

16. Chesterton, *Autobiography*, 102.

17. Oddie, *Romance of Orthodoxy*, 241.

18. Chesterton, *Autobiography*, 154.

19. Ibid., 159, 154.

20. Ibid., 166.

a keen observer of his times, not merely its ideals but how people related to them. What Chesterton noticed about many of his contemporaries was that they liked to have their ears tickled, going to hear lectures by speakers whose claim to fame was their set of unconventional principles. And thus audiences imbibed whatever was new, like sheep "bleating eagerly in whatever neighbourhood it was supposed that a shepherd might be found."[21]

While at university Chesterton was drawn to Christ, not yet as savior but as a person whose love of humankind and particularly the poor became for Chesterton a halfway house between his youthful theological liberalism—Jesus as greatest human who ever lived—and his mature orthodoxy—Jesus as liberator of his soul. What moved him out of this limbo was a growing feeling of gratitude: "that even mere existence, reduced to its most primary limits, was extraordinary enough to be exciting."[22] Jesus became the font and focus of his gratitude:

> There was a man who dwelt in the east centuries ago,
> And now I cannot look at a sheep or a sparrow,
> A lily or a cornfield, a raven or a sunset,
> A vineyard or a mountain, without thinking of him;
> If this be not to be divine, what is it?[23]

Even in this pre-conversion stage of his life, Chesterton found that the "isms" and "ologies" of his time clashed violently with each other, "destroying any sane or rational idea of secular ethics."[24] But when he dwelt on Christianity he discovered "that the old theological theory seemed more or less to fit into experience."[25] To help him think through these incongruities he wrote a book, *Heretics* (1905), in which he challenged his readers to reconsider their opinions about the leading thinkers of the day. To Chesterton modernist thought was less appetizing than it was thin gruel: the ideal of progress had in fact devoured concern about humanity. Thus it was that Friedrich Nietzsche's notion of the death of God generated a nihilism that led not to the joy of freedom but moral paralysis; skepticism bred such uncertainty that its devotees were no better at thinking than the inhabitants of the vegetable kingdom. It was not dogmatism that led to bigotry,

21. Ibid., 170.
22. Ibid., 96.
23. Pearce, *Wisdom and Innocence*, 29.
24. Chesterton, *Autobiography*, 173.
25. Ibid., 171.

Chesterton wrote, reversing course on his earlier stance; rather, "In real life people who are most bigoted are the people who have no convictions at all."[26]

Challenged by a reviewer to write not what he disbelieved but what he held to be true, Chesterton three years later published *Orthodoxy*, which argued that Christian belief, summarized in the Apostles' Creed ("as understood by everybody calling himself Christian until a very short time ago and the general historic conduct of those who held such a creed"), "would be found to be a better criticism of life than any of those I had criticized [in *Heretics*]."[27] Having made determinism orthodoxy and free will heresy, secularists drove Chesterton to understand that bad thought created bad ethics, for secularism produced more not less inhumanity. His search for a truth sufficiently deep to build a meaningful life on had taken him a decade; *Orthodoxy* announced his arrival home.

In the midst of his journey from doubt to belief Chesterton met Frances Blogg, a devout high church Anglican who was very fond of the Bible—and dancing. She was the first person he had ever known for whom religious belief was woven into every aspect of her life, so that intellect and emotion pulled in the same direction. Chesterton dedicated *The Ballad of the White Horse* to her: "I bring these rhymes to you/Who brought the Cross to me."[28] Several years later he met an Anglican curate, Conrad Noel, and as a consequence of these friendships Chesterton, "shifted nearer and nearer to the orthodox side; and eventually found myself . . . in the very heart of a clerical group of canons and curates."[29] What a strange outcome for a former atheist!

Like the scientist testing the hypothesis with data, Chesterton analyzed the props of his paganism and found them intellectually weak and emotionally dry. The determinism of the leading intellectuals of his day led people away from joy, to nothing more than to expect the expected. But as far back as the mid-1890s Chesterton had written in a notebook: "Have you ever known what it is to walk/Along a road in such a frame of mind/That you thought you might meet God at any turn of the path?"[30] The year after he published *Orthodoxy*, Chesterton in a magazine essay made it clear that

26. Chesterton, *Heretics*, 201.

27. Chesterton, *Orthodoxy*, 215; Chesterton, *Autobiography*, 212.

28. Chesterton, *Collected Poems*, 206.

29. Chesterton, *Autobiography*, 165.

30. Oddie, *Romance of Orthodoxy*, 148.

the Christianity he believed in was traditionalist rather than modernist. Orthodox Christianity comprised an unchanging core while nevertheless like a tree at the fringes always grew and changed; the opposite was true for much of modernist Christianity.

These intellectual and emotional elements in Chesterton's conversion were closely connected to his populist political beliefs. He despised the elitism of adherents of new religions, like the ancient Gnostics always demanding "others to rise to the spiritual plane where they themselves already stood . . . they never seemed to hope that *they* might evolve and reach the plane where their honest green-grocer stood."[31] As well he loathed the corresponding elitism of so-called "progressive" thinkers. Chesterton loved the ordinary human, "the old beer-drinking, creed-making, fighting, failing, sensual, respectable man."[32] Any religion that did not find support from such people was in his mind was not worth considering. As he put it in *Heretics*, "Democracy is founded on reverence for the common man."[33] Thus it was that Chesterton's political and religious beliefs were intertwined, combining democracy and orthodox Christianity, so that in his mind "tradition is only democracy extended through time."[34] This produced one of his most famous aphorisms: "Tradition means giving votes to the most obscure of all classes, our ancestors. It is the democracy of the dead."[35]

Two decades after becoming a believer Chesterton had a second transformation: he joined the Catholic Church. What he thought true about Catholic theology was that if a sin were repented of and confessed, the believer truly began over again—as if one could return to one's childhood, as in fact Jesus had proposed. He also believed that the Catholic Church, by defending tradition was "the only champion of reason."[36] The theological liberalism of the Anglican Church disturbed him: "We do not want, as the newspapers say, a Church that will move with the world. We want a Church that will move the world. . . . It is by that test that history will really judge, of any Church, whether it is the real Church or no."[37]

31. Chesterton, *Autobiography*, 146.

32. Chesterton, *Heretics*, 70.

33. Ibid., 186.

34. Chesterton, *Orthodoxy*, 250.

35. Ibid., 251.

36. Chesterton, *Catholic Church and Conversion*, 68.

37. Ward, *Chesterton*, 398.

Calling

Chesterton's conversion to Christianity was critical for pushing him into the public arena, as a journalist, radio commentator, lecturer, and debater who shared a stage with the likes of Bertrand Russell and George Bernard Shaw. Having once entered that arena Chesterton became one of the great public intellectuals of his time. This provided him a platform—literally on some occasions—to take on issues such as eugenics by testing them against orthodox Christianity.

Chesterton understood his vocation as resulting in part from his personality; in his mind he became a journalist "because I could not help being a controversialist."[38] Because at first journalism provided only a meager income, Chesterton worked for a succession of publishers for six years. In this stage of his life after his day job he wrote for hours each evening.

From 1902 until his death Chesterton penned op-ed pieces for three different newspapers. In these thousands of columns one sees his own sense of vocation emerging, which was to champion the little person over elites—whether artistic, political, academic, or scientific—while throwing down as many gauntlets as he could in order to shape public doctrine. "I believe this age wants philosophical arguments, arguments about fundamentals, more than anything," he wrote in a 1903 column.[39] Chesterton was an instinctual democrat when despite democracy being enshrined in the constitution, the newly privileged of pen and pocketbook were undermining the individual capacity to take initiative.

At the point he entered the world of journalism it was rather like the Internet today—something of a Wild West. In an era when journalism did not value honesty Chesterton stood out as a truth teller. He maintained as well the courage of his convictions. Even when he worked for newspapers whose politics he supported he took their foibles to task—and in one case an editor fired him. With his strong commitment to democracy he supported working-class movements, for example unions, even when it was clear that readers were on the other side. It was in fact difficult for his contemporaries to pin him down politically, and scholars today disagree what his politics were, some labelling him a reactionary, others a revolutionary. Chesterton's journalism, if one takes the trouble to read it, built on a core of ideas to which he attached the issues of the day—which makes for some difficulty in

38. Chesterton, *Autobiography*, 277.

39. Coates, *Cultural Crisis*, 76.

comprehending where he's going because of immediate context, but worth-while because in many ways his work transcended the moment.

Faith in the little man was a legacy of Chesterton's own curiosity about his childhood sense of wonder and his love of children. Thus he loved children because of the intersection of his serious and playful sides. Play was serious work and in his serious work he was almost always playful. Nowhere was this truer than in his faith. "Christianity is itself so jolly a thing that it fills the possessor of it with a certain silly exuberance, which sad and high-minded rationalists might reasonably mistake for mere buf-foonery and blasphemy."[40] Chesterton asked, and asks us, "Does your dis-content paralyze your power of appreciating what you have?" If this is the case, then replace displeasure with gratefulness, and find a means to "enjoy enjoyment."[41]

Chesterton was as earnest in contemplating childhood as anything he pondered. In one place in *Orthodoxy* he makes a theological point by con-sidering children, who "because they have an abounding vitality, because they are in spirit fierce and free, therefore they want things repeated and unchanged. They always say, 'Do it again.'" He then adds, "It is possible God says every morning, 'Do it again' to the sun; and every evening, 'Do it again' to the moon. . . . The repetition in Nature may not be a mere recurrence; it may be a theatrical *encore*."[42] He and his wife Frances could not have children of their own, but took delight in the children of friends and relations, telling them stories and drawing pictures for them. And chil-dren loved him. A neighbor in Chesterton's London years recalled, "When I was alone with him, I felt I was an important person worth talking to."[43] In this photograph Chesterton, who is about fifty, draws vitality from what may be understood as his play-mate. Might he be thanking her for what she taught him?

G. K. Chesterton

---

40. Chesterton, *Blatchford Controversies*, 374.

41. Chesterton, *Autobiography*, 323.

42. Chesterton, *Orthodoxy*, 263–64.

43. Ker, *Chesterton*, 164.

Achievements

Sometimes we attain internal clarity as the consequence of a crisis. For Chesterton this came in the form of a 1912 Parliamentary bill promoting eugenics, which became law the following year. I have chosen to focus on one achievement of Chesterton for a number of reasons. Thinking about our bodies is in many ways the greatest interrogative of the last century because it connects to so many others—the spiritual versus the material, the subjective over the objective, rights versus responsibilities, beliefs and behaviors, and the manifestation of a culture of death that stretches from the nihilistic 1890s straight through to our own time. The result is cultural confusion over a critical concern: What—or who—are our bodies for? Working out his belief in Christianity while understanding the importance of limits and the key role played by democracy helped Chesterton construct a coherent worldview, which in turn shaped his stand on the issues of his day great and small, from the poor versus the rich to small nations and peoples versus colonial empires—and, momentously, eugenics. On issue after issue Chesterton was the conscience of his age, establishing the spiritual roots of cultural, political, and economic topics.

Let's listen to one argument in Chesterton's *Autobiography*, published posthumously in 1936 but written over many years, about democracy being worthwhile only if it worked to sustain human dignity. He begins the discussion by stating that, "our industrial civilization [is] rooted in injustice." Chesterton then contrasts his writings with contemporary opinion: "But anybody reading this book (if anybody does) will see that from the very beginning my instinct about justice, about liberty and equality, was somewhat different from that current in our age; and from all the tendencies towards concentration and generalisation." He then links democracy and dignity:

> It was my instinct to defend liberty in small nations and poor
> families; that is to defend the rights of man as including the rights
> of property; especially the property of the poor. I did not really
> understand what I meant by Liberty, until I heard it called by the
> new name of Human Dignity. It was a new name to me; though it
> was part of a creed nearly two thousand years old.

As in almost everything he wrote, here Chesterton revisits the argument that truth was deeply rooted and stable, not reinvented every moment. Finally, he pulls together all these thoughts:

In short, I had blindly desired that a man should be in possession of something, if it were only his own body. In so far as materialistic concentration proceeds, a man will be in possession of nothing; not even his own body. Already there hover on the horizon sweeping scourges of sterilization or social hygiene, applied to everybody and imposed by nobody. At least I will not argue here with what are quaintly called the scientific authorities on the other side. I have found one authority on my side.[44]

That authority made it plain that humans were created in the image of God and drew their meaning from this fact.

Concern about shoddy thinking regarding the human body led Chesterton to condemn the eugenics movement, whose arguments were put forth by many leading intellectual figures of his time in response to a growing fear of racial degeneration. One early expression was an 1873 article by Francis Galton, inventor of the term *eugenics* (from the Greek words "good" and "birth") and a proponent of the theory that inheritance determined personal fitness:

I do not see why any insolence of caste should prevent the gifted class, when they had the power, from treating their compatriots with all kindness, so long as they maintained celibacy. But if these continued to procreate children inferior in moral, intellectual and physical qualities, it is easy to believe the time may come when such persons would be considered as enemies to the State, and to have forfeited all claims to kindness.[45]

The idea was repeated in popular culture, for example in H. G. Wells' 1895 novel *The Time Machine*, which introduced Britons to the feeble-minded Eloi as a future race resulting from racial degeneracy. As a result of eugenist propaganda, by the early 1930s a number of European nations, Canadian provinces, and most American states had put the eugenic ideal into practice by legalizing involuntary sterilization. By the time it was over more than 60,000 North Americans had been sterilized, a disproportionate number of them people of color, poor, and female. The numbers for Sweden and Germany were 40,000 and 400,000.

Chesterton's writings on this topic exhibit a deadly seriousness, suggesting the grave nature of the subject for him. He believed his fellow Britons were unprepared intellectually and morally to confront the ultimate

44. Chesterton, *Autobiography*, 330.
45. Galton, "Hereditary Improvement," 129.

implications of a new eugenics regime as put forward by prophets who by failing to ask themselves tough questions placed humankind at risk. The result would be that too much power over life would be given to the state or a regime of experts which, because they had abandoned traditional moral constraints, would produce "any conceivable or inconceivable extravagances of Eugenics"—in a word, thought Chesterton, "they are simply gambling."[46] This was evident in their language: stock phrases for scientific adventurism—derived from modernist notions such as progress, evolution, and "unfitness"—had replaced human happiness as traditionally understood.

Chesterton may also have understood eugenics as an alternative religion—he was always suspicious of new religions—for it was publicly pronounced as such by Galton, the movement's intellectual godfather, who was quite prepared for experts to play God. An enthusiastic American eugenist even wrote a "creed for the religion of eugenics." Two clauses reveal pseudoscience morphing into pseudoreligion:

> I believe that . . . we . . . should seek to have 4 to 6 children in order that our carefully selected germ plasms shall be reproduced in adequate degree and that this preferred stock shall not be swamped by that less carefully selected.
> I believe in such a selection of immigrants as shall not tend to adulterate our national germ plasm with socially unfit traits.[47]

For Chesterton, the danger of a religion that was experimental rather than authoritative was that it would have no limits.

> The Eugenist doctors . . . do not know what they want, except that they want your soul and body and mine in order to find out. . . . All other established Churches have been based on somebody having found the truth. This is the first Church that was ever based on not having found it.[48]

"Freeing" the minds of men and women from the constraints of dogma would only produce enslavement to what was ephemeral. Accepting traditional authority, however, had the opposite effect: "Whenever we look through an archway, and are stricken into delight with the magnetic clarity

---

46. Chesterton, *Eugenics and Other Evils*, 395, 349.

47. http://mulibraries.missouri.edu/specialcollections/exhibits/eugenics/davenport.htm.

48. Chesterton, *Eugenics and Other Evils*, 347.

and completeness of the landscape beyond, we are realizing the necessity of boundaries."[49] Have you ever watched a film being shot? If we gaze at the entire set we see too much to make sense of the action, but if we were to look at the director's monitor we see only what the camera is filming and what we will eventually witness in the movie theatre. Was Chesterton on to something, that limits allow imagination?

The movement Chesterton attacked had two wings. Negative eugenics sought to discourage, institutionalize, or even sterilize those it deemed unfit so as to prevent them from bearing children. Following upon the 1908 report of the Royal Commission on the Care and Control of the Feeble-Minded, the 1913 Mental Deficiency Act legalized forced detention of those deemed "unfit" if two doctors and a magistrate signed the appropriate form. A "model law" included among those liable to compulsory sterilization not only the mentally "unfit" but epileptics, the blind and deaf, cripples, habitual criminals and inebriates, and dependents—including homeless people, orphans, and the poor.

Positive eugenics, on the other hand, sought to encourage the best and brightest to breed with each other. By the 1920s there was a consensus among geneticists that moral defects and as well as moral character could be transferred genetically—hence human breeding represented good science. It also made for beguiling literature. Here is a segment from a text appended to George Bernard Shaw's witty play, *Man and Superman. A Comedy and a Philosophy* (1903), in which Shaw used Friedrich Nietzsche's concept of a super human:

> That may mean that we must establish a State Department of Evolution, with a seat in the Cabinet for its chief, and a revenue to defray the cost of direct State experiments, and provide inducements to private persons to achieve successful results. It may mean a private society or a chartered company for the improvement of human livestock. But for the present it is far more likely to mean a blatant repudiation of such proposals as indecent and immoral, with, nevertheless, a general secret pushing of the human will in the repudiated direction; so that all sorts of institutions and public authorities will under some pretext or other feel their way furtively towards the Superman.[50]

---

49. Chesterton, "Patriotic Idea," 16–17.
50. Shaw, *Revolutionist's Handbook*, ch. x.

If negative eugenics seems frightening from the history that was to follow, the notion of a human stud farm seems barmy—until we realize that important politicians and thinkers such as Winston Churchill, Theodore Roosevelt, Herbert Hoover, the biologist Julian Huxley (later first director of UNESCO), the presidents of Harvard and Stanford, the philosopher Bertrand Russell, and the economist John Maynard Keynes were all supporters of eugenics. Charles Darwin's son Leonard served as president of Britain's Eugenics Education Society (founded in 1907 and heavily academic in its membership), and in his exhaustive 1926 book *The Need for Eugenic Reform*, the younger Darwin advocated ending public assistance for and incarceration of the unfit who would not agree to sterilization. Marie Stopes, a pioneering campaigner for family planning, used her 1920 book *Radiant Motherhood* to call for the "sterilisation of those totally unfit for parenthood [to be] made compulsory."[51] She went on to argue that steps be taken to purify the race, to "eliminate those sources of defect from the coming generation so as to remove from those who are still to be born the needless burdens the race has carried."[52] In 1935 Stopes attended the International Congress for Population Science in Berlin, held under the auspices of the new Nazi regime; indeed, like a number of the proponents of eugenics, she was a devotee of Adolf Hitler. Meantime Margaret Sanger, who coined the term *birth control* and was the founder of the American Birth Control League, renamed in 1942 Planned Parenthood, whose slogan was "To Breed a Race of Thoroughbreds," wrote that "Birth Control propaganda is thus the entering wedge for the Eugenic educator. . . the unbalance between the birth rate of the 'unfit' and the 'fit' [is] admittedly the greatest present menace to civilization . . . the most urgent problem today is how to limit and discourage the overfertility of the mentally and physically defective."[53]

How might we gauge public opinion on eugenics at this time; that is, how does what intellectuals such as Shaw and Wells believe produce public policy that everyone else is forced to follow? Newly-minted concepts such as "feeble-mindedness" and "mental defective" propounded by an increasing numbers of experts gained control of the public mind. Thus Dr. Maurice Eden Paul, a socialist physician, spoke at a medical conference in 1911, urging sterilization of the "unfit" while simultaneously "trying to guide

51. Stopes, *Radiant Motherhood*, 231.
52. Stopes, *Control of Parenthood*, 208–9.
53. Sanger, "Birth Control Propaganda," 5.

public opinion on the matter."[54] Eugenic discourse drew in humanitarian idealists whose minds could be colonized by pseudoscience because of the separation of science from morality. To Chesterton they might hold "noble and necessary truths," but their grip would be weak, for "Their hearts were in the right place; but their heads were emphatically in the wrong place."[55] This rising crescendo gained the ear of politicians and policy makers, made vulnerable by their sense—as a result of moral panic—that they should do as Pilate did: satisfy the crowd.

Let's listen in on how the debate proceeded, how British and American thinkers who considered themselves humanitarians came to propose a lethal solution to the problem they had invented. George Bernard Shaw fretted over

> millions of poor people, ill fed, ill clothed people. They poison us morally and physically: they kill the happiness of society: they force us to do away with our own liberties and to organize unnatural cruelties for fear they should rise against us and drag us down into their abyss.[56]

Shaw went on to proclaim that, "A great many people would have to be put out of existence, simply because it wastes other people's time to look after them."[57] Dr. Arthur Tredgold, who had been a leading voice on the 1908 Feeble-Minded Commission, an early member of the Eugenics Education Society, and author of *Textbook on Mental Deficiency* (1908), testified that for Britain's 80,000 imbeciles and idiots, "it would be an economical and humane procedure were their existence to be painlessly terminated . . . The time has come when euthanasia should be permitted."[58] W. Duncan McKim, MD, author of *Heredity and Human Progress* (1900), in concluding that "Heredity is the fundamental cause of human wretchedness," followed up by suggesting that "The surest, the simplest, the kindest, and most humane means for preventing reproduction among those whom we deem unworthy of this high privilege [reproduction], is a gentle, painless death." Ominously, he added, "In carbonic acid gas, we have an agent which would instantaneously fulfill the need."[59] Not to be outdone, a New York urologist,

54. *British Medical Journal* (Dec. 16, 1911), 1596.

55. Chesterton, *Autobiography*, 170.

56. Shaw, *Major Barbara*, Act 3.

57. Stone, *Breeding Superman*, 127.

58. Kemp, *Merciful Release*, 135.

59. McKim, *Heredity and Human Progress*, 120, 188, 193.

William J. Robinson authored *Eugenics, Marriage and Birth Control* (1917), and argued that, "The best thing would be to gently chloroform these [unfit] children or give them a dose of potassium cyanide."[60]

In an atmosphere pervaded by hysteria over racial degeneration, in 1927 by an 8–1 decision in *Buck v. Bell*, the U.S. Supreme Court upheld a Virginia law allowing compulsory sterilization of the "mentally unfit." The Buck in the case before the court was an eighteen-year old woman who had been forcibly institutionalized; the court challenge to what had been done to her was brought by several apparently "unscientific" Virginia Christians. Justice Oliver Wendell Holmes wrote in his majority opinion that, "It is better for all the world, if instead of waiting to execute degenerate offspring for crime, or let them starve for their imbecility, society can prevent those who are manifestly unfit from breeding their kind."[61] Harold Laski, a political science professor at the London School of Economics and a prominent socialist who two decades earlier had expressed fear that "as a nation we are faced with racial suicide," wrote Holmes after the 1927 decision: "Sterilise *all* the unfit, among whom I include *all* fundamentalists."[62] The Virginia law was not repealed until 1979.

We might ask, What Would Chesterton Have Done? With as much fervour as wit, he suggested "The people I would lock up would be the strong-minded." Chesterton thought ill-reasoned ideas were revealed by careless language.

> Say to them, "The persuasive and even coercive powers of the citizen should enable him to make sure that the burden of longevity in the previous generations does not become disproportionate and intolerable, especially to the females"; say this to them and they sway slightly to and fro like babies sent to sleep in cradles. Say to them "Murder your mother," and they sit up quite suddenly. Yet the two sentences, in cold logic, are exactly the same.[63]

Chesterton maintained that atheists in general and eugenists in particular liked the passive voice because it seemed less contentious, its subject more inevitable. "Should be" avoids the question, "By whose authority?" In Chesterton's mind "evil always takes advantage of ambiguity."[64] Abstract

60. Robinson, *Eugenics, Marriage and Birth Control*, 74.

61. 274 U.S. 200 (1927).

62. Laski, "Scope of Eugenics," 34; Chase, *Legacy of Malthus*, 316.

63. Chesterton, *Eugenics and Other Evils*, 386, 303.

64. Ibid., 297.

virtues were repeated so often that readers lost the will to ask what a phrase such as "liberty from disease" actually meant. Today might we apply the same question to "population control"? Might it mean heaven on an earth racially purified?

World War I led to a decline in the eugenics impulse. But following the war concerns about unemployment, population, and racial degeneration returned; and thus in 1922—the year after the second International Eugenics Conference—Chesterton published *Eugenics and Other Evils*, gathering earlier newspaper writings with reflections on the then current renewal of interest in eugenics. His thoughts also appeared in fictional characters he created, as in the case of Dr. Hentry in *The Return of Don Quixote* (1927): "In plain words, somebody," in this instance various bureaucrats, "was going to treat the eccentric as a lunatic."[65] It turns out one of these officials, Dr. Gambrel, having theorized that brain trouble arose from sitting on the edge of chairs, which Hentry did, carries him off to a hearing before a magistrate. But by an absurd sequence of events Gambrel, "a mad doctor [who] was madder than the madman"[66] is the one institutionalized. Utterly foolish thinking produced an irrational outcome.

For Chesterton, eugenics encouraged a new, destructive morality and at the same time contributed to the then current impulse to expand the power of the state and elites beyond what was either reasonable or safe. "I do not deny, but strongly affirm, the right of the State to interfere to cure a great evil," Chesterton argued. But, regarding eugenics, he went on, "I say in this case it would interfere to create a great evil."[67] Intellectual anarchy would result because there would be no limit to what terms such as "unfit" and "weak-minded" meant: "Anarchy is that condition of mind or methods in which you cannot stop yourself. . . . It is this inability to return within rational limits after a legitimate extravagance that is the really dangerous disorder."[68]

In criticizing eugenics Chesterton asked a series of questions. Firstly, who should make decisions in a realm of life hitherto untouched by forces beyond the individual? Since there was no unified opinion regarding the "unfit," like Dr. Gambrel "each man would have his own favourite kind of

65. Chesterton, *Return of Don Quixote*, 100–101.

66. Ibid., 218.

67. Chesterton, *Eugenics and Other Evils*, 307.

68. Ibid., 310.

idiot,"[69] and therefore vagueness of language and bad science produced less than useless statistics. Chesterton's query quoted the language of the 1913 Mental Deficiency Act, about those "incapable of managing their affairs with proper prudence." He characterized such word choice as unreasonable:

> [T]he aim of the measure is to prevent any person whom these propagandists do not happen to think intelligent from having any wife or children. Every tramp who is sulky, every labourer who is shy, every rustic who is eccentric can quite easily be brought under such conditions as were designed for homicidal maniacs.[70]

Stated otherwise, Chesterton wanted to constrain a new, pseudoscientific authority by limiting the power of the recently installed experts, in effect by using the universal morality of humankind: "And as he has no moral authority to enforce a new conception of happiness, so he has no moral authority to enforce a new conception of sanity."[71] Chesterton posed the case of marrying into a family with consumption (tuberculosis), which at the time was thought to be hereditary and thus fodder for negative eugenists. "The sickness or soundness of a consumptive may be a clear and calculable matter. The happiness or unhappiness of a consumptive is quite another matter, and is not calculable at all."[72] Somehow Chesterton knew the theory was mistaken, based on "our broken knowledge and bottomless ignorance of heredity."[73]

This consideration led Chesterton to another. As the eugenist could only suggest himself as the authority, the result would be the tyranny of the expert. Thus he issued tirades—against magistrates, judges and especially "the highly placed and highly paid experts."[74] He insisted that, "A man is not an imbecile if only a Eugenicist thinks so." Other than the insane, in Chesterton's experience "one man is not so widely different from another."[75] Is this our experience? Recall such people to mind—a neighbour, a member of your family, a classmate of your children. Was Chesterton right?

Third, Chesterton raised the concern about human dignity. Terming any person "unfit" displayed contempt for humanity. Regarding the

69. Ibid., 329.

70. Ibid., 308.

71. Ibid., 322, 348.

72. Ibid., 324.

73. Ibid., 340.

74. Ibid., 313.

75. Ibid., 319–20.

feeble-minded, in "the few cases I know well they are not only regarded with human affection, but can be put to certain limited forms of human use."[76] Chesterton proposed that common sense should trump the regime of experts, arguing narrowly that "no scientific man must be allowed to meddle with the public definition of madness," and more broadly that "Through all this modern muddle there runs the curious principle of sacrificing the ancient uses of things because they do not fit in with the modern abuses."[77] Unreasonable thinking leads to madness, just as poor laws led to lawlessness.

Finally, Chesterton argued that the eugenics movement produced injustice because it was prejudiced against the poor. The case for a "plutocratic impulse behind all Eugenics"[78] is evident in the books, pamphlets, and articles of the proponents of eugenics themselves. When Chesterton asked, who really benefitted from the eugenics regime, his answer was the wealthy and powerful, those disinclined to limit their motivation by a regimen of social justice for the poor, thus producing a war on the weak. The prominent journalist Arnold White had expressed concern in his 1901 pro-eugenic book, *Efficiency and Empire*, about "the asylums maintained by the ratepayers . . . a vast plant of machinery for infecting the next generation."[79] Late Victorian and early twentieth-century language notwithstanding, the poor were not a race but individual souls with their own stories.

As well as secular-minded modernists Chesterton crossed swords with liberal Christians such as the Anglican dean of St. Paul's, W. R. Inge, who wished for a "Christian-Biological morality" (perversely, he used for support Matthew 5:48, "Be ye therefore perfect, even as your Father in heaven is perfect") and E. W. Barnes, bishop of Birmingham, who also pronounced that eugenics was in accordance with God's plan: "Christianity . . . tries to make what we may call a spiritually-eugenic society. It recognises that by no means all human beings are fit for this society. 'Many are called but few are chosen' is a saying of its Founder." Sterilization was the preferred solution to degenerates breeding freely, thought Barnes, because they were "an impediment to the creation of what the Christian terms the Kingdom of God on earth."[80]

76. Ibid., 328, 334, 386.
77. Ibid., 406–7.
78. Ibid., 389.
79. White, *Efficiency and Empire*, 110.
80. Inge, "Moral Aspects of Eugenics," 33; Barnes, "Eugenics and Religion," 11, 14.

If ever a case needed to be made for a historic and contextualized rather than a contemporary and individualistic reading of the Bible, this is it: Did Inge not read three chapters later in St. Matthew's Gospel, "Inasmuch as you have done it to one of the least of these my brothers, you have done it to me"? (Matt 25:40) For his part Barnes hoped, though Christians were "very conservative," that nevertheless they could be enlightened: "If you could demonstrate that the feeble-minded were not only in themselves a social burden but also that there was nothing in them of value to the race you would rapidly win Christian sympathy and support."[81] It was troubling to Chesterton that liberal Christians could be found making the same arguments as non-believers, and as one historian suggests were the eugenics movement's most enthusiastic supporters.[82] Would Chesterton be similarly distressed today? The point, then and now is that protection, not destruction of the weak has always been an essential element of Christianity. Here is the prophet Isaiah on God: "He won't break a bruised reed. He won't quench a dimly burning wick. He will faithfully bring forth justice" (Isa 42:3).

Although not as prominently discussed in his own autobiography nor in most of the scholarship on Chesterton and conspicuously absent from surveys of early twentieth-century British history, his campaign against eugenics was an important element of Chesterton's stand against the spirit of his age, and for orthodox Christianity as the antidote to modernist ideologies. Because the debate over eugenics vexed Chesterton intellectually and morally—as a bad idea it would lead to bad ethics—in *Eugenics and Other Evils* Chesterton proposed a revolutionary response to the danger at hand: "we are already under the Eugenist State; and nothing remains to us but rebellion."[83] For Chesterton, revolution was defined as turning back to recover the things lost. This "turning back" is what believers understand by repentance.

During his lifetime what may have been Chesterton's impact on this challenge? It is always easier to assess the positive impact of a thinker than the negative. Nevertheless, it is what did *not* happen that must be noted: Britain was the only industrialized European state not to turn to eugenics, and Chesterton's voice cannot be discounted. After the First World War fear that a growing number of "mental defectives" would overwhelm the

81. Barnes, "Eugenics and Religion," 17.

82. Wilkinson, "Politics of the Anglican Modernists."

83. Chesterton, *Eugenics and Other Evils*, 308.

nation's racial stock resulted in renewed scientific arguments for negative eugenics. But in 1931 the House of Commons defeated a bill which would have permitted sterilization of the unfit. Attempts by a committee of inquiry in 1932–34 comprising committed eugenists failed to generate a royal commission and in turn new legislation. The British public was no longer panicked about racial degeneration; eugenics was an idea whose time had passed. The opinions and mode of argument in *Eugenics and Other Evils* appear repeatedly in academic work on the debate on eugenics in Britain in the 1930s even though their source is almost never acknowledged. And there is clearly a direct line from Chesterton's arguments to the preamble of the 1948 United Nations *Universal Declaration of Human Rights*: "[R]ecognition of the inherent dignity and of the equal and inalienable rights of all members of the human family is the foundation of freedom, justice and peace in the world."[84] In his own time and place Chesterton stood almost alone against eugenics, for which we should be grateful.

Chesterton challenged modern thinking about the body by showing what that thinking would lead to. As a Catholic he would probably turn over in his grave if he heard me suggest that he was essentially a Calvinist regarding the believer's cultural mandate, for he frequently referenced the importance of limits while chiding eugenists to "leav[e] the rest to God."[85] But throughout his writings he pressed readers to love the world while at the same time trying to change it. Thus already in 1903 he put it simply in a newspaper editorial: "If we let go the old superstition of Charity, do not let us fancy there will not be new philosophies to step into its place; vast, shapeless and inhuman philosophies."[86] Three decades later the Nazis came to power in Germany, and with a vengeance applied their pernicious understanding of "racial degeneracy."

Chesterton understood the critical weaknesses of the various parts which made up the modernist package of ideals—materialism, evolution, skepticism, progress, determinism, worship of the will and of the state—as well as atheism and new religions, all of which he saw as insufficiently tough-minded to address what was wrong with the world. In short, only God should play God. Today we likewise face assaults on human dignity—including abortion on demand, most perversely sex-selective abortion, growing calls for euthanasia, human genetic engineering, unrestrained

84. United Nations, "Universal Declaration of Human Rights."

85. Chesterton, *Eugenics and Other Evils*, 300.

86. Coates, *Cultural Crisis*, 82.

embryonic stem cell research, cloning, and assisted suicide. China's one-child policy produces forced late-term abortions and sterilization. And at the farthest edge of this mode of thinking there's transhumanism, a movement which seeks to reengineer the human body to forestall its decay and death, to create a techno sapiens to replace homo sapiens. Philosophically this is Superman; anyone who has read Nietzsche or Shaw knows we have been here before; any historian will, unhappily, tell you what happened as a consequence. While new in the sense of its dependence on discoveries in biotechnology, the movement can be traced intellectually back to the eugenists and to the very issues raised by Chesterton in defense of human nature.

Strip away the language of boosterism, the worship of the autonomous individual, the images of heroic scientists fighting armies of obscurantists, strip away all the promises of diseases to be cured and progress to be achieved and what is left is what Chesterton saw as evil: this is the story told by a culture of death, one of whose weapons is the hastening of evolution so that those humans will now take control of what has been progressing too slowly.

These problems remind us of the essential role played by Christians in confronting the idols of the age. Chesterton, like other believers, was imperfect. He ate took much, and he drank too much, which in 1914 along with his sedentary life almost killed him. In his own words he was "a poor fallen but baptized journalist."[87] But he provides a model for taking up the challenge of this chapter, claiming that

> The Christian ideal has not been tried and found wanting. It has been found difficult; and left untried. . . . Men have not got tired of Christianity; they have never found enough Christianity to get tired of.[88]

Chesterton was a truth-teller in an age of false prophets. We can read him today for pleasure—in particular his way with words. But we would be wiser to hear Chesterton again or for the first time on what makes us matter.

87. Chesterton, *Eugenics and Other Evils*, 307.
88. Chesterton, *What's Wrong With the World*, 61, 65.

His text

Instead of looking at books and pictures about the New Testament I looked at the New Testament. There I found an account, not in the least of a person with his hair parted in the middle or his hands clasped in appeal, but of an extraordinary being with lips of thunder and acts of lurid decision, flinging down tables, casting out devils, passing with the wild secrecy of the wind from mountain isolation to a sort of dreadful demagogy; a being who often acted like an angry god—and always like a god. Christ had even a literary style of his own, not to be found, I think, elsewhere; it consists of an almost furious use of the *a fortiori*. His "how much more" is piled one upon another like castle upon castle in the clouds. The diction used about Christ has been, and perhaps wisely, sweet and submissive. But the diction used by Christ is quite curiously gigantesque; it is full of camels leaping through needles and mountains hurled into the sea. Morally it is equally terrific; he called himself a sword of slaughter, and told men to buy swords if they sold their coats for them. That he used other even wilder words on the side of non-resistance greatly increases the mystery; but it also, if anything, rather increases the violence. We cannot even explain it by calling such a being insane; for insanity is usually along one consistent channel. The maniac is generally a monomaniac. Here we must remember the difficult definition of Christianity already given; Christianity is a superhuman paradox whereby two opposite passions may blaze beside each other. The one explanation of the Gospel language that does explain it, is that it is the survey of one who from some supernatural height beholds some more startling synthesis.

G. K. Chesterton, *Orthodoxy* (1908)

Questions

1. Are there lessons from how Chesterton worked through his spiritual crisis? That is, how did his mind change?

2. What was the basis for Chesterton's argument against eugenics? What larger general principle was he advocating?

3. Do you agree with Chesterton that in order to prevent both inhumanity and tyranny, *expertise* must be in conversation with *common sense*?

4. Chesterton believed, "When it comes to life the critical thing is whether you take things for granted or take them with gratitude." How would you respond to him were he to ask how you are doing in this regard?

5. How might Chesterton's arguments be applied today to issues regarding what the body is for?

For further reading

Chesterton, G. K. *Autobiography* (1936). In *The Collected Works*, vol. xvi. San Francisco: Ignatius, 1988.

———. *Eugenics and Other Evils* (1922). In *The Collected Works*, vol. iv. San Francisco: Ignatius, 1987)

———. *Orthodoxy* (1908). In *The Collected Works*, vol. i. San Francisco: Ignatius, 1986.

Ker, Ian. *G. K. Chesterton: A Biography*. Oxford: Oxford University Press, 2011.

Chapter 7

Dorothy Sayers

Story: Makers—Whose work is it?

And before everything let us not forget
that to do good it is necessary first to do well.
Dorothy Sayers, age 62

"THE ONLY CHRISTIAN WORK is good work, well done."[1] That aphorism defines the calling of its creator, Dorothy L. Sayers, teacher, publisher's assistant, copywriter for an advertising firm, novelist, poet, scholar, essayist, playwright, social critic, theologian, vamp, unwed mother, devout Anglican, churchwarden of her London parish. In an unconventional life that began in the early 1890s and ended in the late 1950s, Dorothy Sayers managed to be all of these and much more. Today she is best-known for her novels featuring an aristocratic amateur detective. For an older generation, Sayers was a pioneering religious broadcaster, whose 1940s BBC radio serial, *The Man Born to Be King*, brought the words of Christ into their living rooms. She was a friend of the Oxford-centered Christian writers known as the Inklings, and was famous among British feminists for her essay, "Are Women Human?"

In many ways a troubled life, hers was also an examined one—hence the value of studying Sayers's reflection on what work is. A lay theologian, she was a believer who took seriously the task of integrating faith and her

1. Sayers, *Creed or Chaos*, 108.

multiple vocations, encouraging fellow believers to make their work excellent, challenging her contemporaries to become perceptive Christians, and calling the church to spell out a theology of vocation—to "include within her sacraments all arts, all letters, all labour and all learning."[2]

It often takes time to figure out what work one is supposed to do. I only understood my calling while working on my PhD. Later I noticed as a professor that many students came to me not with concerns about course content but about what they might do after graduation. It was in the middle of my career, as my own calling was changing, that I first encountered Dorothy Sayers's *The Mind of the Maker*, a book about work as a creative activity. It was tough going: she was a brilliant writer whose novels and essays are easy reads, but when addressing a theological subject Sayers expected readers to work hard at getting her. It was only the third time through the book, when I read it with a student whose insights told me she could be a Sayers for the twenty-first century, that I finally understood what the author was getting at. As I went on to read almost everything else Sayers wrote I discovered that no matter what genre she worked in, from plays to novels, from books and essays to private letters, sooner or later she got to the subject of work. As this topic is so very vexing for many of us, in this chapter I want to have her help us take work apart and put it back together.

Sayers confronted the banality that Christianity was essentially about how one felt rather than what one thought, countering that it was "hopeless to offer Christianity as a vague, idealistic aspiration: it is a hard, tough, exacting, and complex doctrine steeped in drastic and uncompromising realism."[3] In terms of creative artists like her, Sayers believed inadequate thinking produced mediocre art: "A loose and sentimental theology begets loose and sentimental art-forms; an illogical theology lands one in illogical situations; an ill-balanced theology issues in false emphasis and absurdity."[4] By extension her tough-minded approach applied to all who work by hand or mind, hence her challenge to us: think about how we might cultivate a sacred understanding of work, and it will change forever how we comprehend what we do.

Born in 1893, Dorothy Leigh Sayers was the daughter and grand-daughter of Church of England clergymen. Sayers recalled that while her

2. Sayers, "Church's Responsibility," 67.

3. Sayers, *Creed or Chaos*, 44.

4. Sayers, *Man Born to Be King*, 13.

childhood was "hedged about . . . with moral restrictions,"[5] these were never harshly applied. An only child, she was with her parents a great deal, and at school and university her letters home contained far more intimate details of her life than one would expect from a person who in the future so valued her privacy.

Sayers was first taught at home. Her father, a one-time school headmaster, began to instruct her in Latin when she was six, and she learned French and German from a governess. Boarding school followed, where she felt like a fish out of water because of her intellect, her remarkable skills in languages and creative writing, and her dislike of sports—all unusual for women in school culture at the time.

From her earliest days Dorothy Sayers exhibited a fondness for writing in all genres. Her first novel did not appear until she was thirty, but when just thirteen she wrote and produced a play, while in her early twenties she published a book of poetry. Creative writing, whether financially rewarded or not, was to be her vocation, but the road to realize that was a long one.

After boarding school, having won a scholarship, Sayers entered Oxford, becoming one of the first women to receive a degree from the university. At Oxford she studied modern languages and continued to write poetry. Sayers succeeded at Oxford not because she worked hard but because she was brilliant. Having learned how to learn, she spent a great deal of time doing what she wanted to do: "It's not exactly that I am idle," she wrote a friend, "but I'm interested in something else the whole time."[6] Besides writing, that included flirting with a variety of men, taking care about her clothes, singing, dancing, and boating. Another female Oxford student at the time recalled her as "A bouncing and exuberant young female who always seemed to be preparing for tea parties."[7] And yet looking back Sayers recalled that her Oxford years were when she acquired what defined the rest of her life, the "habit of intellectual integrity."[8]

Following Oxford it took her quite some time to discern her vocation. Like so many young people who thoroughly enjoyed their college years, her nostalgia about that time lingered: "I *do* want Oxford! If I've not got a job which keeps me stuck elsewhere this autumn I shan't be able to keep

---

5. Sayers, *Letters*, iii., 423.

6. Ibid., i., 77.

7. Brittain, *Testament of Youth*, 105.

8. Reynolds, *Sayers*, 252.

away from the place."[9] She went on to hold teaching positions on three occasions, but only when there were no alternatives. Acceptance of a permanent teaching job would be to admit defeat as a writer. One of her students overheard her saying, "I'd rather sweep streets than teach children."[10] She wrote her parents, appraising the classroom and her subsequent work at a publishing house: "I'm sure writing is much more my job than office work or teaching. Big classes of youthful people are not in my line."[11] At first then Sayers only knew what she was not meant to do.

"I can't get the work I want,"[12] she complained to her mother in 1921. Two years later, when she was thirty, she had already held four jobs but had yet to sort out her vocation, as evident in her haste to quit positions. During these years Sayers went through some experiences she did not discuss much, in effect beginning to compartmentalize her private and public lives. Having turned down one suitor, she fell in love with another man who eventually rejected her. Subsequently she engaged in a passionate affair that broke her heart when it ended—once again not on her terms. Then at thirty-one Sayers had an illegitimate son by another man, with whom she was not in love. Her aged parents were never told the truth, nor were her friends. While in some manner having a child was an act of creation and thus fulfilling for her, for professional and privacy reasons she could not have him live with her, and the boy was brought up by a cousin. Sayers struggled emotionally to leave behind the guilt over what she had done, in spite of an intellectual comprehension that "Evil can never be undone, but only purged and redeemed."[13]

Two years after her son's birth, aged thirty-three, Sayers married a journalist, a divorced, wounded, and psychologically scared veteran of World War I whose two children were raised by their mother. As her career rose his declined; the friction that ensued was exacerbated by her husband's refusal to have Sayers's son live with them. While the marriage survived until her husband's death, Sayers's early ideals for a meaningful life partner were never realized. It was in work that she found an outlet for her passion.

9. Sayers, *Letters*, i., 110.

10. Reynolds, *Sayers*, 74.

11. Sayers, *Letters*, i., 190.

12. Ibid., i., 178.

13. Brown, *Seven Deadly Sins*, 303.

Conversion

The faith that Dorothy Sayers eventually made her own developed in stages intertwined with both private life and public career. Broken-hearted by affairs, the long-distance relationship with her son, her unrewarding marriage, and flummoxed by her constantly changing jobs, understandably Sayers's faith did not take final form until she reached some capacity of stability in her life. Because she was such a private person and so prized the life of the mind, Sayers left little record of the development of her faith. Appropriately, for her case, I'm going to play the role of detective and sift through the few clues she left behind. Here's the critical question I want to engage: did her faith extend beyond an intellectual assent to doctrine and creed?

Her clergyman father she recalled as religious but not inclined to instruct his daughter in Christian doctrine. During her childhood she held to the formalities of faith rather than developing a relational spirituality. At school after declaring she was an agnostic Sayers began to be attracted to an intellectually-grounded Anglo-Catholicism, which she maintained throughout her life. In one letter to her parents Sayers remarked, "I am so glad you've got *Orthodoxy*. I am not surprised to hear that that [G. K.] Chesterton is a Christian. I expect though, that he is a very cheerful one and rather original in his views, eh?"[14] Her remarks reveal that she had read enough of Chesterton's other writings to have found a cerebral comrade. After his death in 1936 Sayers told Chesterton's widow: "G. K.'s books have become more a part of my mental makeup than those of any other writer you could name."[15]

While at boarding school Sayers was confirmed in the Church of England. In writing to her mother soon after about classmates who were taking communion together on Easter Sunday, she admitted that "being at school, one feels rather out of it if one doesn't do things *with* the school."[16] Although not expressing displeasure at the time about her confirmation, at thirty-seven she wrote a cousin that the experience was worse than being baptized against her will, for it created "resentment against religion which lasted a long time. The cultivation of religious emotion without philosophic

---

14. Sayers, *Letters*, i., 18.
15. Ibid., i., 394.
16. Ibid., i., 40.

basis is thoroughly pernicious—in my opinion."[17] Between her late teens and late thirties, then, something changed. In effect, she had worked out her salvation. One sign is in a letter when Sayers was in her early twenties, written to a friend planning to enter the teaching profession, about "gawky young souls growing out of their spiritual clothing, like mine was when I was at school."[18] *Belief* for Sayers had to be a marriage of head and heart, best understood in a phrase of hers—"the passionate intellect."[19]

Except in letters to her parents, she rarely wrote anything regarding her feelings about faith. Was it because for her faith was strictly a private matter? Was it because as an intellectual she didn't like enthusiasm when she saw it in others? Looking back years later Sayers recalled a "secret rapture" when she would hear, in Latin, these words from the opening line of the Athanasian Creed: "Whosoever would be saved."[20] In an unpublished autobiographical novel she wrote when she was forty, the heroine Katherine sometimes communicates in the same words Sayers used in her letters. In one instance Katherine speaks wistfully of an alternative to mere enthusiasm: "In the book called *Orthodoxy* there were glimpses of this other Christianity, which was beautiful and adventurous and queerly full of honour." Sayers went on: "A strict course of exact and dogmatic theology might well provide the intellect with a good, strong bone to cut its teeth on; but . . . to worship with the understanding had already, in Katherine's schooldays, become unfashionable."[21] Considering this evidence it seems Sayers's faith was in flux during her schooldays, but was moving toward a passionate intellectual belief in God.

At Oxford Sayers attended church but corporate worship was not the center of her life. Her efforts to forge an intellect that could discern truth about the world from counterfeit evidence was helped by reading Chesterton's *What's Wrong with the World* (1910). But when an Oxford friend tried to enlist her in a campus Christian organization Sayers refused:

> The only necessary products of Christianity are those which Christ appointed. He did not encourage misty theological discussion, but taught by authority and by example. The early Christians did the same. . . . The C.U. [Christian Union] appears to me more like a

17. Ibid., i., 306.
18. Reynolds, *Sayers*, 58.
19. Sayers, *Letters*, iv., 141.
20. Ibid., iv., 154.
21. Reynolds, *Sayers*, 41.

product of Darwinism. Yes—you must aggressively save souls, but you will never do it by unprofitable argument. . . . Christianity rests on Faith, not Faith on Christianity. If you have read *Orthodoxy* you will see what I mean.[22]

Although later Sayers told a cousin about a phase in her life when she disowned Christianity, it was emotional expression she distrusted. When twenty-three she told her parents: "I do not at all mind discussing my soul—I do it every day—but I do not like doing it with very earnest people of narrow experience."[23] An early employer recalled a crucifix was always on her desk and that she said grace at meals, while a friend noted she was "so bloody religious."[24] In 1918, when at age twenty-five she published a second book of poems, *Catholic Tales and Christian Songs*, she wrote to her parents that "I can assure you that it is intended at any rate to be the expression of reverent belief, but some people find it hard to allow that faith, if lively, can be reverent."[25] Lively did not countenance enthusiasm.

Nor would Sayers put up with an individualistic worldview that dispensed with dogma—the historic Christian community's understanding of its faith. Reading the Bible using deep theological reflection and thorough awareness of historic context nurtured communitarian rather than individualistic acuity. In her 1946 play, *The Just Vengeance*, a pilot killed in combat returns to post-war Britain; struggling to understand the meaning of justice given what he has been through, he adopts a personal creed—to which an angel responds: "Did you think you were unbegotten?/ Unfranchised? With no community and no past?"[26]

Looking back from the end of her life it is possible to see Sayers the creative writer and Sayers the believer growing in tandem. At some point she had come to believe that what the Bible says is true. Christianity, she wrote in 1952, "is not primarily an emotional experience, or a set of logical conclusions, or a code of ethics: it is a *story*. It is not constructed out of man's feelings or reason or even his moral imperatives. It is the story of God's act in history."[27] One either joined a community that believed that story and acted on it, or the individual believed some alternative story.

22. Sayers, *Letters*, i., 72.

23. Ibid., i., 85.

24. Reynolds, *Sayers*, 80.

25. Sayers, *Letters*, i., 138.

26. Sayers, *Four Sacred Plays*, 295.

27. Simmons, *Creed Without Chaos*, 49, n. 11.

Two other episodes reveal the contours of her belief. In 1943 the Archbishop of Canterbury wanted to confer on her a Doctor of Divinity degree. She would have been the first woman so honored, but Sayers replied that she didn't deserve the degree. Her reasoning reveals that she separated out belief and vocation in what may not have been healthy, a lingering guilt from her earlier life, as well as circumspection—which was beneficial.

> But I have only served Divinity, as it were, accidently, coming to it as a writer than as a Christian person. A Degree of Divinity is not, I suppose, intended as a certificate of sanctity, exactly; but I should feel better about it if I were a more convincing kind of Christian. I am never quite sure whether I really am one, or whether I have only fallen in love with an intellectual pattern.[28]

Then near the end of her life, when challenged by a fellow Christian intellectual because she didn't bother to evangelize, Sayers responded: "I am quite without the thing known as 'inner light' or 'spiritual experience.' . . . I am quite incapable of 'religious emotion.'" She went on, thinking along the lines of her spiritual mentor Chesterton: "Of all the presuppositions of Christianity, the only one I really have and can swear to from personal inward conviction is sin. About that I have no doubt whatever and never have had." And then she added autobiographically: "Since I cannot come at God through intuition, or through my emotions, or through my 'inner light' (except in the unendearing form of judgement and conviction of sin) there is only the intellect left. . . . Where the intellect is dominant it becomes the channel of all the other feelings. . . . I don't know whether we can be saved by the intellect, but I do know that I can be saved by nothing else."[29]

What, then do these clues reveal about the development of her life as a believer? As time went on, Sayers applied faith to her work and work to her faith. Looking back she described herself as always a Christian "insider," but in fact it took her decades to make the faith her own. In her early twenties she wrote to her parents: "It's difficult to make people see that what you have been taught counts for nothing, and that the only things worth having are the things you find out for yourself."[30] That had apparently happened while she was at Oxford, both in affirming her own spiritual inclinations as formed by her intellect—that Christianity was true—and simultaneously rejecting alternatives derived from feelings or intuition. This sentiment

28. Sayers, *Letters*, ii., 429.
29. Ibid., iv., 137–38.
30. Ibid., i., 85.

recalls her friend C. S. Lewis's advice in *Mere Christianity*: "The battle is between faith and reason on one side and emotion and imagination on the other."[31] Sayers never tells us when for her that battle was won. Appropriately for a writer of detective fiction, this will always remain something of a mystery. But once won, she openly spoke to others about what she believed, writing to a friend when she was in her mid-forties about a discussion over sherry with a nominal Christian: "I always seem to be expounding the Faith in pubs!"[32] The same was true about her writing: it was "the educated near-Christians or woolly Christians that we write for. *They* are our people and the sheep of our pastures."[33]

There is this promise in the biography of Jesus written by his follower John, that everyone who believes in the name of Christ will be given the right to become children of God (John 1:12). Repentance reflects a changed mind. Did Sayers's mind change? Only by looking back from the end of her life is the answer to this question a definitive yes. One of my faculty colleagues, who grew up in Latin America, recently conveyed to me that in her culture it was easier to talk about one's sex life than one's faith. So it was for Dorothy Sayers.

Calling

As we have already seen, for Sayers the path of discovering what she was supposed to do was a convoluted one. The early phase of her life might be thought of as her quest for calling. During World War I she had applied to train as a nurse but had been turned down, as she was for a position in government work. Forced by her financial situation, she was compelled to teach off and on. The longest held paying job Sayers ever had was as a copywriter for London's largest public relations firm. She enjoyed Benson's Advertising Agency for its creativity and camaraderie—as is evident in her 1933 mystery novel *Murder Must Advertise*—but from the beginning had misgivings about the effect of her work: she wrote regarding her first production, "It is all lies from beginning to end."[34] Advertising ceased being intellectually satisfying and by her mid-thirties she was complaining that the work at Benson's was getting in the way of her writing. As she suggested for

31. Lewis, *Mere Christianity*, book 3, ch. 11.
32. Sayers, *Letters*, ii., 68.
33. Ibid., iv., 144.
34. Ibid., i., 192.

others so for herself: the criteria were that the work one did must be both well done and well intentioned. Here we see the conflict between her career and who Sayers was as a person—and so at the end of 1929, still in her mid-thirties, she left Benson's. This second phase, which might be termed the quest for success, took Sayers from her late twenties to her mid-forties.

That she had found her calling in writing—both as means (theology) and end (creativity)—is suggested by her output and, as Sayers noted to a friend at the time, her understanding that "My proper job is making things with my imagination."[35] During 1923–28, while still working at Benson's, Sayers published four novels, twelve short stories, and edited a volume of detective tales. What may seem at first frivolous work, writing novels was an opportunity to take on serious concerns, such as the problem of evil, but also a chance to employ her ingenuity. Thus were her novels works of intellect and acts of creation.

Reading her life alongside her fiction shows that Sayers often wrote about her own experiences after she had had time to digest their meaning and attach them to big ideas. By her late thirties, well into her career as a novelist, she began to connect Christian doctrine to the problems of her times. Consider this portrait painted when Sayers was in her mid-fifties. If

one looks closely at the original in London's National Portrait Gallery, it seems she turns away from her project on the table to speak to us. Her left eye looks out at the world, while the right eye looks at the viewer. With a wry smile she might be saying to the observer, "My novels and plays will entertain you, but be careful when reading them. I'm going to challenge you regarding the problems that beset us."

After fourteen years which saw the publication of a dozen detective novels and a number of short stories, Sayers reached the end of what she could do with her character in terms of addressing the great concerns of her time. She then turned to creating plays and overseeing their staging, writing essays and books on theology and other subjects, and in her last years research and scholarship on the medieval Italian poet Dante Alighieri. This represents a new understanding of her calling, producing a phase that lasted until her

Dorothy Leigh Sayers
By Sir William Oliphant Hutchison
© National Portrait Gallery, London

35. Reynolds, *Sayers*, 237.

death in 1957 at age sixty-three. Sayers' dramatic work had been triggered by a request to write a play which came in turn via Charles Williams, a fellow author who knew her heart and mind. As in the case of many people, Sayers was thus aided in perceiving her vocation by discerning friends.

Rather like her experience at Benson's, the corporate aspect of theatrical production complemented her creative side. Sayers's publications during this time also reveal an increased zeal for orthodox theology. In a 1941 letter she complained, "I hate having my intellect outraged by imbecile ignorance and by the monstrous distortions of *fact* which the average heathen accepts as being 'Christianity.'"[36] Given when in her life this shift happened suggests that she, like others, having tasted success and found it insufficient, turned to significance as her life's purpose. There's a clue in her second to last novel, *Gaudy Night*, which dealt with a number of moral problems, including integrity in work and relationships. At one point the character Harriet Vane in *Gaudy Night* states, "To be true to one's calling, whatever follies one might commit in one's emotional life, that was the way to spiritual peace."[37] A letter Sayers wrote to her publisher concerning the novel suggests that commentary had replaced entertainment as her objective: "It is the only book I've ever written which embodies any kind of a *moral* and I do feel rather passionately about this business of the integrity of the mind." Sayers recognized the problems inherent in using a detective story as the vehicle for applying Christian theology to concerns of contemporary civilization. However, she concluded, "It's the book I wanted to write,"[38] suggesting she understood writing novels had become a means rather than an end.

Then there's the clue in *Mind of the Maker* (1941), published four years after her final novel. She observed that readers found detective fiction satisfying because it took their minds off their troubles. Reality, however, "love and hatred, poverty and unemployment, finance and international politics,"[39] is not at all like solving the puzzle of the body in the library. Yet the process of writing detective fiction, however disconnected from reality, had allowed Sayers to discover that work was at its core a creative activity, and, appropriately, as a lay theologian she wrote creatively on work.

36. Sayers, *Letters*, ii., 310.
37. Sayers, *Gaudy Night*, ch. 2.
38. Sayers, *Letters*, i., 357.
39. Sayers, *Mind of the Maker*, 188–89.

When in her forties Sayers as transitioned from writing novels, she began explicitly addressing the topic of work. Using a variety of platforms, she pointed out ethical shortfalls in the modern world's economic, industrial, marketing, and distributive systems—and by extension any creative or intellectual product of the human mind and hands—as these encouraged over-consumption. That the church had failed to provide a robust alternative to the secularization of vocation was evident to Sayers when she asked, "Are you and I in the least sincere in our pretense that we disapprove of Covetousness?"[40]

Having worked in an advertising agency for nine years Sayers was particularly well placed to criticize consumerism centered on advertisement as cultural propaganda. She used pointed language to decry "advertisements imploring and exhorting and cajoling and menacing and bullying us to glut ourselves with things we do not want, in the name of snobbery and idleness and sex-appeal."[41] In her 1933 novel *Murder Must Advertise*, those who write copy for an advertising firm never buy the products they promote!

How did Sayers discern this vocation? In the end she came to her calling because very few others could: "The people who are up-to-date in their theology can't write English, and the people who can write English are either untheological or have only a sketchy impression of nineteenth-century liberal-humanist ethics mixed up with a lot of outmoded 'higher criticism.'"[42] Well aware of her own shortcomings, she set out to work out a theology of work.

Achievements

Sayers came to believe that the most fundamental question facing humanity was how to think about work. Her unease about her generation's attitudes may be traced back to the lines in a poem she wrote when she was twenty-three: she gave God thanks "for the joy of labor done" while regretting the "shame of labor lost."[43]

The crux of her concern was that modern people had forgotten they were created by a Creator in order to create, and that therefore the end of humanity's productive energy was the same as God's—to serve creation.

40. Sayers, *Creed or Chaos*, 136.

41. Ibid., 92.

42 Sayers, *Letters*, ii., 300.

43. Reynolds, *Sayers*, 365.

(Chesterton in his *Autobiography* had written: "Only to make things! There is no greater thing to be said of God Himself than that he makes things."[44]) Forgetfulness resulted in misunderstanding work as the means to fund consuming. Doctors habitually ignored the point that the end of medicine is healing, lawyers that the purpose of law is justice, and so forth, resulting in a soulless indifference to work except for its market value. Sayers had seen this in movies: "When we go to the cinema and see a picture about empty-headed people in luxurious surroundings, do we say: 'What drivel!' or do we sit in a misty dream, wishing we could give up our daily work and marry into surroundings like that?"[45] Looking backward, although her tone was often shrill, Sayers had in fact discerned the shape of things to come. As we look around today, consider this comment of hers: "The commodities easiest to sell after the labour-saving gadgets are the inventions for saving us from the intolerable leisure we have produced, and for painlessly killing the time we have saved."[46] As my granddaughter might say, busted!

If the amount we are paid for our work is the only criterion of success, we can never be satisfied because there is no end to wanting things. As an alternative, Sayers found it helpful to think about our attitude toward activities for which we receive no monetary reward, for example hobbies. When we consider these we find them rewarding and the products good even though we are paid nothing for them. In this case, Sayers suggested, the worker "is no longer bargaining with his work, but serving it."[47] She noted that it took crises such as the Great Depression and World War II to realize that a monetary standard of success was inadequate. It is in such contexts that we observe how vital it is to establish the integrity of the work as more important than money, worldly success, or a shallow understanding of happiness.

Work, then, is not what we do to live, but what we live to do. A new set of questions should therefore arise. Of an enterprise, not will it pay but is it good? Of people, not what do they make but what is their work worth to society? Of goods, not can we get people to buy them but are they useful and well made? Of a job, not what's the salary but will it use my gifts?

Believers understand that they serve God in their work. Sayers might say to both scholar and student that such service happens in a well-crafted

---

44. Chesterton, *Autobiography,* 50.

45. Sayers, *Creed or Chaos,* 137.

46. Sayers, "Vocation in Work," 136.

47. Sayers, *Creed or Chaos,* 102.

paper as much as in or even before we nurture the homeless—particularly if we are in the habit of doing the latter in lieu of the former. The church should therefore avoid promoting a spiritual hierarchy of vocations. Neither should it tolerate bad architecture, music, sermons, or publications, for we do not honor God when we aim no higher than mediocrity.

Work for Sayers was not an aspect of life we do so that or until we can escape to do something else, such as leisure. Humans need to be freed to—not freed from—work, evident in the dialogue between two angels in Sayers's 1937 play, *The Zeal of Thy House*:

> Cassiel: "Happily, being an angel, and not a man, I like work. The hatred of work must be one of the most depressing consequences of the Fall."
>
> Gabriel: "Some men work like angels—and whistle over their work. They are much the most cheerful kind."[48]

Those who most hate their work are not necessarily just the underpaid or workers who do physically taxing labor or perform drudgery. Work-lovers often carry on exacting work for which they are not well-paid, as in the case of the sailor who is restless when on dry land. For Sayers, therefore, the only valid measure of success is doing well work that needs doing.

Having once written, "Capitalist or Communist, I cannot believe that salvation is to be found in any system which subordinates Man to Economics,"[49] Sayers insisted that a more sacramental concept of work served as an antidote for any social system based on the vices of avarice or envy. In our time such systems have produced *homo economicus* and collectively societies characterized by greed and waste because we treat striving for an ever higher standard of living as a virtue.

The first information we have concerning creation, in the opening lines of the Bible, points to the ideal of the joy-filled worker. God created, and seeing everything made, including humans, concluded, "It was very good." From the first chapter of Genesis Sayers derived creative activity as the fundamental quality God and humans share: the "creative mind is in fact the very grain of the spiritual universe."[50] After reflecting on how Sayers suggested we determine what work each of us is to do, I want to return

48. Sayers, *Four Sacred Plays*, 13.

49. Sayers, *Letters*, ii., 160.

50. Sayers, *Mind of the Maker*, 185.

to this matter of creative activity, for it is her most original contribution to a theology of vocation.

Work for Sayers ought to be centered on calling, "the full expression of the worker's faculties, the thing in which [man] finds spiritual, mental, and bodily satisfaction, and the medium in which he offers himself to God."[51] Christianity could lay the groundwork for lives that were full of life, not by freeing humanity *from* work but rather *to* work and to work well.

Writing was to be Sayers's calling; if anyone was destined to write, she was. Calling is, however, much more than acceptance of one's destiny. The person called needs to add discernment, to choose what she shall become. In the case of Dorothy Sayers this involved evenings at the British Museum doing research on criminology so that her novels had integrity—all the while maintaining her day job at the advertising agency.

Calling is not without challenges. For Sayers the difficulties were first in discovering what she was meant to do, and then protecting her calling from fellow Christians. Sayers was particularly irritated by clergy who preached the importance of discerning vocation "when at the same time they try to take me away from my vocation, which is to be a craftsman with words, to waste my time doing something for which I have no vocation and no talent, merely because I have a name."[52] If the good is indeed the enemy of the best, then doing well is in permanent tension with doing good.

By now, most readers should be asking what all this means for those who are not creative artists. Although we were all made by God in order to create, relatively few of us are gifted authors like Dorothy Sayers. *Work* for Sayers was broadly defined, however, extending well beyond creative writing. Far more than most intellectuals, she felt drawn to common people. Sayers constantly observed artisans and others who labored, asking them questions, and wondering whether there were other methods that might function better. She sought to make her thinking on work universally applicable because as the result of creation, creativity was inherent in all humans and thus there was no distinction in that regard between a laborer and an artist.

In "Living to Work," a radio broadcast written after World War II and aimed at a general audience, she stressed that work should promote the opportunity for individual initiative, allow workers to see the fruit of their labor, and correspond to the natural rhythm of life. Consequently, Sayers

51. Sayers, *Creed or Chaos*, 101.
52. Guinness, *The Call*, 180.

made a case against factory work. She did not believe that factory workers could not love and serve their work, but that in general factories removed creativity by essentializing efficiency. A consequence of the industrial age, the lost connection between labor and product created workers more concerned with pay than with, in her words, the "honesty, beauty, and usefulness of the goods produced." Sayers suggested that workers should be matched to work instead of forcing them to dedicate their lives to "making badly things which were not worth making."[53]

According to Sayers, misinterpretation in how contemporary society viewed work breeds thriftless consumption and social indifference. With a right understanding of work, the misconception disappears that the most spiritual vocation for a Christian is becoming a missionary or pastor, therefore validating all types of work humanity has at its fingertips. Engage in creative, lively, fulfilling work. Work, and work well. It is what the Creator created you for.

Sayers believed that such a conception of work helps maintain equilibrium between vocation and the life of the believer. This is further clarified when she addresses the problem of integrity. The place to begin is by considering human freedom in light of the two greatest commandments. For Sayers, true freedom was not freedom from external restrictions but freedom to be true to our real nature. Only with integrity regarding the first great commandment might one attempt to fulfill the second.

These concerns appear in Sayers's third novel, *Unnatural Death*. A minor character, Vera Findlater, discusses how she construes a relationship: "It's got to be just everything to one. It's wonderful the way it seems to colour all one's thoughts. Instead of being centered in oneself, one's centered in the other person." Findlater then adds, in what turns out to be tragic irony: "That's what Christian love means—one's ready to die for the other person." Findlater is only a few degrees off course, for did not Jesus say, "No one has greater love than to give one's life for one's friends" (John 15:13)? Findlater's sentimental theology was criticized by another character, Alexandra Climpson, who learned from a sermon that "that kind of love might become *idolatry* if one wasn't very careful. . . . One must get the *proportions* right."[54] Ignoring Climpson's advice, Findlater then lies to protect her friend, that is, she puts the second commandment higher than the first—and in a premeditated act is later murdered by this very friend.

53. Sayers, *Creed or Chaos*, 105.

54. Sayers, *Unnatural Death*, ch. xvi.

As Sayers pointed out elsewhere, we serve our community best by serving God first, that is, by disregarding the community to focus on the work. "It is the work that serves the community; the business of the worker is to serve the work."[55] As Climpson cautioned Findlater about integrity in personal relationships, Sayers warned her contemporaries about being taken in by the phrase, *serving the community,* suggesting it was "the slogan of every commercial scoundrel and swindler who wants to make sharp business practice pass muster as social improvement."[56] To scoundrels and swindlers she might have added totalitarian rulers.

The Climpson character also reminds us about balancing spiritual priorities and work. She wrote her employer Lord Peter Wimsey that the vicar at the parish she was visiting "teaches sound Catholic doctrine," so she could attend his church (which she needed to do to seek clues), "without doing *violence* to my religious beliefs—a thing I could *not* undertake to do, even in your interests."[57] Integrity demands we refuse work we must not do even were we to be paid for it, realizing that we could not do the work honestly or well.

Sayers addressed integrity powerfully in *The Devil to Pay* (1939). For this play she created a Faust for an interwar audience, who anticipates both modern socialists and televangelists in his goal, "the promise to do away with toil and labour, with poverty, pain and suffering, and to ensure to every man health, wealth and long days upon the earth."[58] Her Faust speaks the language of secularism by questioning God's goodness and claiming for himself a calling to free humanity from "the burden of fear and pain and poverty that God has laid upon you."[59] As a consequence he mistakes his vocation for that of Jesus. This imbalance between means and ends not only results in personal confusion but social chaos as well. Scene III witnesses what follows from attempts to be good without God: Faust creates not utopian bliss but battlefield slaughter. The same man who set out to cure social ills ends by finding joy in war as entertainment, because when challenged to follow Christ he comments, "That way is too long and uncertain."[60] This theme is reminiscent of the scene in *Unnatural Death,*

---

55. Sayers, *Creed or Chaos,* 114.

56. Ibid., 111–12.

57. Sayers, *Unnatural Death,* ch. iv.

58. Sayers, *Two Plays About God and Man,* 53.

59. Ibid., 57.

60. Ibid., 60.

where Vicar Tredgold tells Lord Peter, who speculates whether euthanasia may be appropriate in some circumstances, "It's not our business."[61] Sayers reminds us that modern people have the unfortunate habit of playing God rather than performing their own work.

If balance and integrity in work and relationships are worthy ends, Sayers thought pride is foremost among the vices that would destroy them. She characterized pride as "the sin which proclaims that Man can produce out of his own wits and his own impulses and his own imagination the standards by which he lives: that Man is fitted to be his own judge." In her mind pride was "pre-eminently the sin of the noble mind," a form of corruption which created more evil than all other vices.[62] Pride was often personified in Sayers's fictional villains—invariably through perversion of a character's calling.

Based on a historic event, her 1937 play *The Zeal of Thy House* explores this problem of hubris. The play opens as the brothers of Christchurch, Canterbury are choosing the architect to rebuild the cathedral's choir after an 1174 fire. Three men are being considered: a local man of faith, an economical builder, and William of Sens, a highly talented foreigner. (If you were on the search committee, which would you choose?) Although William is certainly the most gifted architect, questions arise about his moral character. His life is at odds with his creative excellence: William plays loose with the truth, has devouring ambition, cuts corners, but does exceptional work, to which he is dedicated (perhaps too much so, for at one point he states, "Sometimes one has to damn one's soul for the sake of the work"[63]). In William we come face to face with the fatal temptation that the work is ours alone. Thus there are two simultaneous issues in the play that join, as Sayers was later to write her son, in a single concern: Is what we make more important than what we are?

In a conversation with the prior, one of the brothers calls William "a man without truth," to which the prior replies, "All of the truth of the craftsman is in his craft." The brother counters by saying that he "would rather have a worse-built church with a more virtuous builder."[64] The prior voices Sayers's conviction about the spiritual nature of work: God gave William skills and calling, thus it would be cheating God to choose a second-rate

61. Sayers, *Unnatural Death*, ch. xix.
62. Sayers, *Creed or Chaos*, 150–51.
63. Sayers, *Four Sacred Plays*, 31.
64. Ibid., 59–60.

architect. The prior wins the argument, and William is commissioned to direct the work.

The play turns on a speech made by William: "We are the master-craftsmen, God and I—/We understand one another." Because William creates he assumes he knows how God felt during creation: "He loved the work, as I love mine, And saw that it was good, as I see mine." Regarding human creative workers William remarks that they "like God can call beauty from dust, Order from chaos, and create new worlds."[65] Having started down this path of worshiping the creation, William cannot turn back. With each step he moves closer to disaster. First he proposes equality of God and humankind as creators: "In making man God over-reached Himself and gave away his Godhead. He must now depend on man . . . Man stands equal with Him now." Then equality gives way to unmitigated pride, for regarding Canterbury, William remarks, "This church is mine, And none but I, not even God, can build it." When his companion Ursula is shocked by these words William responds:

> He knows that I am indispensable
> To His work here; and for the work's sake, He,
> Cherishing, as good masons do, His tools,
> Will keep me safe.

As the angels comment, "the ungodly is trapped in the work of his own hands."[66]

The climax comes when a terrible accident leaves the architect crippled. William's dreams have turned into nightmares. He is troubled by a sense of guilt but still driven to complete his work, believing only he can finish it—that he is still indispensable. Confessing to the sin of pride following a dream wherein the Archangel Michael helps him understand his real problem was in his attitude to the work, William has finally come to understand that even Christ left his work for others to carry on. He acknowledges

> But let my work, all that was good in me,
> All that was God, stand up and live and grow.
> The work is sound, Lord God, no rottenness there—
> Only in me.[67]

---

65. Ibid., 69.
66. Ibid., 72.
67. Ibid., 99.

And so William leaves Canterbury to return to his native France, telling the distraught workers that he is not the only architect in the world. The more gifted the worker, the more difficult it is to make such a declaration. In creating *Zeal of Thy House* Sayers understood how gratitude for the Incarnation—God becoming human—was the only antidote to the pride inherent in creative persons.

As she aged Sayers's contrarian side strengthened: she was a spiritual being in an increasingly secular age, a thinker in an increasingly consumerist age; she championed personal choice and freedom in an age increasingly interventionist and statist; and she was a traditionalist in an increasingly modern age. Sayers comprehended that modern learning—with its fragmented worldview, compartmentalizing aspects of life—inculcated the opposite of integrative thinking. "I have no use whatever for Enlightened Opinion," she pronounced, "whose science is obsolete, its psychology superficial, its theology beneath contempt and its history nowhere."[68] It should be no surprise to us that Sayers was turned down by a government agency during World War II, one representative commenting, "very difficult and loquacious."[69] But she was faithful, joining an Anglican organization which encouraged writing to soldiers. Being Dorothy Sayers she whimsically reflected on her letters' recipients: "that to be harangued about religion by a middle-aged female must add very greatly to the horrors of war for these helpless and unhappy young men."[70]

Our dilemma is that if Sayers was right, are we not doomed to failure and frustration unless we achieve the uncompromising break she proposed? Hence the often strident tone of her critique of the church: cease trying to adapt Christ to humans, rather conform humans to Christ; change the world *not* by identifying with worldly affairs but by teaching the world spiritual standards. Like Chesterton, Sayers accused the modern church of attempting to uphold a particular standard of ethical values that derived from Christian truths while gradually dispensing with the very dogmas that were the rational foundation for these values. The root cause of the church's failure to influence the lives of her contemporaries was, she insisted, not that too much stress had been placed on dogma but that it had been neglected or watered down.

68. Sayers, *Unpopular Opinions*, 105.
69. Brabazon, *Sayers*, 172.
70. Ibid., 188.

Because Sayers believed so strongly in this, in the mid-1940s—when she was in her fifties—she became deeply involved in the work of St. Anne's House in London's West End, chairing the council that managed a study center where agnostics and believers engaged in discussions about the Christian faith. This was evangelism on her terms, giving intellectuals and artists "an opportunity of hearing an orderly exposition of the Christian Faith and of asking as many questions as they like and having those questions intelligently discussed and answered."[71]

In *Zeal of Thy House* the prior remarks that God chose as the founder of his church the lying, cowardly, impetuous Peter over John the beloved disciple who knew God's mind. The play points out two errors regarding work: we either make too much of it, hurtling toward idolatry, or too little, accepting mediocrity. From poems, plays, novels, essays, books, and letters Sayers asks us: Whose work is it? That same apostle Peter asked concerning our lives: Who gets the glory? Both questions are satisfied by the prior in *Zeal of Thy House*: "Where there is truth, there is God; and where there is glory, There is God's glory too."[72] Oswald Chambers put it this way: "It is the work that God does through us that counts, not what we do for Him."[73]

Towards the end her life Dorothy L. Sayers wrote that "When we go to Heaven all I ask is that we shall be given some interesting job and allowed to get on with it. No management; no box-office; no dramatic critics; and an audience of cheerful angels who don't mind laughing."[74] I for one look forward to discovering what she has been up to.

71. Sayers, *Letters*, iii., 203.
72. Sayers, *Four Sacred Plays*, 59.
73. Chambers, *My Utmost for His Highest*, August 30.
74. Reynolds, *Sayers*, 371.

Her text

Christianity is, of course, not the only religion that has found the best explanation of human life in the idea of an incarnate and suffering god. We might, therefore, prefer not to take this tale too seriously—there are disquieting points about it. Here we had a man of Divine character walking and talking among us—and what did we find to do with him? The common people, indeed, "heard him gladly"; but our leading authorities in Church and State considered that he talked too much and uttered too many disconcerting truths. So we bribed one of his friends to hand him over quietly to the police, and we tried him on a rather vague charge of creating a disturbance, and had him publicly flogged and hanged on the common gallows, "thanking God we were rid of a knave." All this was not very creditable to us, even if he was (as many people thought and think) only a harmless crazy preacher. But if the Church is right about him, it was more discreditable still; for the man we hanged was God Almighty.

So that is the outline of the official story—the tale of the time when God was the underdog and got beaten, when he submitted to the conditions he had laid down and became a man like the men he had made, and the men he had made broke him and killed him. This is the dogma we find so dull—this terrifying drama of which God is the victim and hero.

If this is dull, then what, in Heaven's name, is worthy to be called exciting? The people who hanged Christ never, to do them justice, accused him of being a bore—on the contrary; they thought him too dynamic to be safe. It has been left for later generations to muffle up that shattering personality and surround him with an atmosphere of tedium.

To those who knew him, however, he in no way suggested a milk-and-water person; they objected to him as a dangerous firebrand. True, he was tender to the unfortunate, patient with honest inquirers and humble before Heaven; but he insulted respectable clergymen by calling them hypocrites; he referred to King Herod as "that fox"; he went to parties in disreputable company and was looked upon as a "gluttonous man and a wine-bibber, a friend of publicans and sinners"; he assaulted indignant tradesmen and threw them and their belongings out of the Temple; he drove a coach-and-horses through a number of sacrosanct and hoary regulations; he cured diseases by any means that came handy, with a shocking casualness in the matter of other people's pigs and property; he showed no proper deference for wealth or social position; when confronted with neat dialectical traps, he displayed a paradoxical humor that affronted serious-minded people, and he retorted by asking disagreeably searching questions that could not be answered by rule of thumb. He was emphatically not a dull man in his human lifetime, and if he was God, there can be nothing dull about God either. But he had "a daily beauty in his life that made us ugly," and official-dom felt that the established order of things would be more secure without him. So they did away with God in the name of peace and quietness.

"And the third day he rose again"; what are we to make of that? One thing is certain: if he was God and nothing else, his immortality means nothing to us; if he was man and no more, his death is no more important than yours or mine. But if he really was both God and man, then when the man Jesus died, God died too, and when the God Jesus rose from the dead, man rose too, because they were one and the same person.

Dorothy Sayers, "The Greatest Drama Ever Staged" (1938)

Questions

1. Like others, having tasted success and found it insufficient, Sayers turned to significance as her life's purpose. What can we learn from her in this regard?

2. How might better comprehending *work* help us understand who we are as humans? For example, ponder Sayers's suggestion: "As we *are* so we *make*."

3. Why, like Chesterton, did Sayers not trust the experts—in this case economists?

4. "The worker's first duty is to serve the work." Why did Sayers believe that this is a better approach than serving the community, which is usually the first instinct of a believer?

5. "The only Christian work is good work, well done." Too easy? Too unrealistic?

For further reading

Coomes, David. *Dorothy L. Sayers: A Careless Rage for Life*. Oxford: Lion Publishing, 1992.

Reynolds, Barbara. *Dorothy L. Sayers: Her Life and Soul*. New York: St. Martin's Griffen, 1993.

Sayers, Dorothy L. *The Letters of Dorothy L. Sayers*, 4 vols. Edited by Barbara Reynolds. New York: St. Martin's, 1996–2000.

———. *The Mind of the Maker*. New York: HarperSanFrancisco, 1987. Online: http://www.worldinvisible.com/library/dlsayers/mindofmaker/mind.c.htm

Conclusion

Did Believers Make a Difference?

It is communion with others across the ages
that is more sorely needed today
than even communion with others in our time.
Charles Malik, *The Two Tasks*

SELINA HASTINGS WAS BORN in 1707; Dorothy Sayers died in 1957. In those two and a half centuries Britain, by all accounts hardly an example of a Christian nation, became one. This, at least, is the view of an outsider, one who agrees with Oswald Chambers that there really isn't such a thing as a "Christian nation."[1] Both as historian and pilgrim I'm far more intrigued by the impact of believing people on their neighbors, their nation, and the world. If we reflect on the subtitle of this book, what's the evidence that a handful of believers made a difference in modern Britain?

In an essay published early in the twentieth century, G. K. Chesterton pronounced that, "In the end it will not matter to us whether we wrote well or ill . . . It will matter to us greatly on which side we fought."[2] In this he seems to be reflecting an argument made by the medieval theologian Thomas à Kempis: "On the Day of Judgment we shall not be asked what we have read, but what we have done."[3] Which side did these eight mere believers fight on? If we were to ask them, what have you done, how would they answer?

1. Chambers, *Utmost for His Highest*, October 16.
2. Chesterton, *All Things Considered*, 11.
3. Kempis, *Imitation of Christ*, book 1, ch. 3.

One way to approach these questions is to ask yourself whether you heard the name Selina Hastings before reading this book. What about Olaudah Equiano, or Biddy Chambers? What about the term, *eugenics*? Based on the audiences that have heard me discuss the subjects of *Mere Believers* over the years my guess is many of these stories were unfamiliar. Nevertheless, as moderns we believe what they achieved. That fact is one answer to the question of whether or not they made a difference.

Another might come from bearing in mind Chesterton's argument against eugenics. The summer prior to putting the finishing touches on this book I re-met a colleague teaching at a research university; for purposes of anonymity I'll call him Rick. In the midst of a presentation he was making I asked him how he came to do the research he does, which concerns how institutions serve people with developmental disabilities. Rick told the following story: When he was in college at a prestigious southern university, by a process so convoluted it could not possibly have happened by chance, he spent a summer as a counselor at a camp whose residents were men and women with developmental disabilities. One of them, an intellectually disabled man, led Rick to Christ. Do all people matter, or do some of us matter more than others who can thus be ignored—or worse? We know how Chesterton would answer that.

Imagine sitting at a table with Selina Hastings, Olaudah Equiano, Hannah More, William Wilberforce, Oswald and Biddy Chambers, G. K. Chesterton, and Dorothy Sayers. It's not hard to imagine that sparks could fly between Hastings, the Chambers, and Chesterton over the merits of Calvinism. But what I find most salutary about these eight believers is that having accepted the offer of grace there was no instance of a will to power in their lives. So I rather suspect that around that table they would be encouraging one another, because that's what they did while they were alive: The Countess of Huntington and Hannah More encouraged Olaudah Equiano; Equiano and More encouraged William Wilberforce; G. K. Chesterton encouraged Biddy Chambers and Dorothy Sayers.

Here's the tableau of the neighborhoods and nations that comprise the world of past, present, and future, which the Bible refers to as the kingdom of heaven, as a consequence of the contributions of our eight believers. They might be thought of as culturally-wise rebels who fought as they did because they were able to look beyond their own eras, to "fix [their] eyes not on what is seen, but on what is unseen, since what is seen is temporary, but what is unseen is eternal" (2 Cor 4:18).

- The Countess of Huntington: a denomination, a seminary, those churches in Africa, the creation of a theologically-informed female not at all afraid of being a leader.

- Olaudah Equiano: demonstrating ethnic equality, the creation of a man of color who rose above his cultural context.

- Hannah More: the poor educated because they were people, the creation of a society woman who used her creative gifts to go beyond her social script.

- William Wilberforce: the idea of a world without slaves, the creation of a man who understood his calling was public.

- The Chambers: the realization of freedom from self, the creation of integration of spirit and intellect.

- G. K. Chesterton: challenging do-gooders who promoted exploiting the human body, the creation of a mind who understood the true meaning of human dignity.

- Dorothy Sayers: arguing our work must be well done, the creation of a mind capable of thinking well beyond what work was.

What then does *believer* call forth? The chapters revealed remarkably thoughtful people who, less than perfect beings, struggled with finding faith. And then having done so, in some cases it took years of trial and error to determine, given their gifts, what they were called to do. For each of them there were paths taken or experiences undergone or setbacks suffered that could have led to defeat. But these developments bestowed a concentration of courage in the application of calling to their times—even in the face blistering criticism—that I, frankly, envy.

I also appreciate the remarkable comradeship exhibited in these eight lives. If we were therefore to ask, What does *Christian community* call forth?, the answer appears to be something like this: engage with others, both in thinking and in doing. Might I, might we, have similar perseverance in fixing on the work needing doing, and doing faithfully and well. And in so discharging our individual callings, how many of our neighborhoods and nations might flourish?

Select Bibliography

Adeane, Jane H. *The Early Married Life of Maria Josepha, Lady Stanley*. London: Longmans, Green, 1899.

Ashe, Katherine. *The Book of the College: An Account of the Bible Training College 1911–1915* (Unpublished: 1915).

Aspinall, Arthur. *The Letters of Princess Charlotte, 1811–1817*. London: Home and Van Thel, 1949.

Barnes, Ernest. "Some Reflections on Eugenics and Religion." *Eugenics Review* 18 (April 1926–January 1927) 7–14.

Barrett, James W., and P. E. Deane. *The Australian Army Medical Corps in Egypt*. London: Lewis, 1918.

Belmonte, Kevin. *Hero for Humanity: A Biography of William Wilberforce*. Colorado Springs: NavPress, 2002.

Boswell, James. *The Life of Samuel Johnson*, 6 vols. Edited by L. F. Powell. Oxford: Clarendon, 1934.

Brabazon, James. *Dorothy L. Sayers: A Biography*. New York: Scribner, 1981.

Brittain, Vera. *Testament of Youth*. New York, Macmillan, 1933.

Brown, Janice. *The Seven Deadly Sins in the Works of Dorothy L. Sayers*. Kent, OH: Kent State University Press, 1998.

Burke, Edmund. *First Letter on a Regicide Peace* (1796). In *The Writings and Speeches of Edmund Burke*, 9 vols, edited by R. B. McDowell, vol. 9, 187–264. Oxford: Clarendon, 1981.

Carretta, Vincent. *Equiano, the African: Biography of a Self-Made Man*. New York: Penguin, 2006.

Chambers, Biddy. *Oswald Chambers: His Life and Work*. London: Oswald Chambers Publications Association, 1959.

Chambers, Oswald, *Afterward*. In *Oswald Chambers: Abandoned to God*, by David McCasland, 310. Grand Rapids: Discovery House, 1993.

————. *The Complete Works of Oswald Chambers*. Grand Rapids: Discovery House, 2000.

————. "How the Blessing Came." *Spiritual Life* 58 (March 1949) 4–5.

————. *Insane* (1893). In *Oswald Chambers: Abandoned to God*, by David McCasland, 295. Grand Rapids: Discovery House, 1993.

————. *My Utmost for His Highest*. Westwood, NJ: Barbour, 1963.

————. *The Place of Help* (1935). In *The Complete Works of Oswald Chambers*, by Oswald Chambers, 982–1058. Grand Rapids: Discovery House, 2000.

————. *Prayer Pleading* (1901). In *Oswald Chambers: Abandoned to God,* by David McCasland, 315. Grand Rapids: Discovery House, 1993.

————. "With God at the Front" (March 18, 1917). In *The Complete Works of Oswald Chambers,* by Oswald Chambers, 1039–41. Grand Rapids: Discovery House, 2000.

Chambers, Oswald. Papers, SC–122. Wheaton College Archives and Special Collections, Wheaton, Illinois.

Chase, Alan. *The Legacy of Malthus: The Social Costs of the New Scientific Racism.* New York: Knopf, 1977.

Chatterton, Georgiana. *Memorials, Personal and Historical of Admiral Lord Gambier.* London: Hurst and Blackett, 1861.

Chesterton, G. K. *All Things Considered.* Henley-on-Thames, UK: Finlayson, 1969.

————. *Autobiography* (1936). In *The Collected Works of G. K. Chesterton,* vol. xvi. San Francisco: Ignatius, 1986–.

————. *The Blatchford Controversies* (1904). In *The Collected Works of G. K. Chesterton,* vol. i. San Francisco: Ignatius, 1986–.

————. *The Catholic Church and Conversion* (1927). In *The Collected Works of G. K. Chesterton,* vol. iii. San Francisco: Ignatius, 1986–.

————. *The Collected Poems of G. K. Chesterton.* New York, Dodd, Mead & Co., 1932.

————. *Eugenics and Other Evils* (1922). In *The Collected Works of G. K. Chesterton,* vol. iv. San Francisco: Ignatius, 1986–.

————. *The Everlasting Man* (1925). In *The Collected Works of G. K. Chesterton,* vol. ii. San Francisco: Ignatius, 1986–.

————. *Heretics* (1905). In *The Collected Works of G. K. Chesterton,* vol. i. San Francisco: Ignatius: 1986–.

————. *Orthodoxy* (1908). In *The Collected Works of G. K. Chesterton,* vol. i. San Francisco: Ignatius, 1986–.

————. *The Outline of Sanity* (1926). In *The Collected Works of G. K. Chesterton,* v. San Francisco: Ignatius, 1986–.

————. "The Patriotic Idea." In *England: A Nation,* edited by Lucian Oldershaw, 1–43. London: R. Brimley Johnson, 1904.

————. *The Return of Don Quixote* (1927). Philadelphia: Dufour, 1963.

————. *Tales of the Long Bow* (1925). In *The Collected Works of G. K. Chesterton,* vol. viii. San Francisco: Ignatius, 1986–.

————. *What's Wrong With the World* (1910). In *The Collected Works of G. K. Chesterton,* iv. San Francisco: Ignatius, 1986–.

Christian, Martha [Marsha Drake]. *Searching for Mrs. Oswald Chambers.* Carol Stream, IL: Tyndale, 2008.

Coates, John D. *Chesterton and the Edwardian Cultural Crisis.* Hull, UK: Hull University Press, 1984.

Cobbett, William. *Parliamentary History of England,* 36 vols. London: Hansard, 1806–1820.

Colley, Linda. *Britons: Forging the Nation, 1707–1837.* New Haven: Yale University Press, 1992.

Cook, Faith. *Selina, Countess of Huntingdon.* Carlisle, UK: Banner of Truth Trust, 2001.

Cormack, Patrick. *Wilberforce: The Nation's Conscience.* Basingstroke, UK: Pickering and Inglis, 1983.

Cowper, William. *The Minor Poems of William Cowper.* London: G. Offor, 1818.

D'Arbley, Frances Burney. *Diary and Letters of Madame d'Arbley,* 7 vols. Edited by Charlotte Frances Barrett. London: H. Colburn, 1842–1846.

Doddridge, Philip. *Diary and Correspondence,* 5 vols. Edited by John Humphreys. London: H. Colburn and R. Bentley, 1831.

Edwards, Paul, and Rosalind Shaw, "The Invisible *Chi* in Equiano's *Interesting Narrative.*" *Journal of Religion in Africa* 19 (1989) 146–56.

Einstein, Albert, et al. *Living Philosophies.* New York: Simon and Schuster, 1931.

Elgood, P. G. *Egypt and the Army.* London: Oxford University Press, 1924.

Equiano, Oladuh. *The Interesting Narrative of the Life of Olaudah Equiano.* Edited by Robert J. Allison. Boston: Bedford, 1995.

Ferguson, Niall. *Empire: The Rise and Demise of the British World Order and the Lessons for Global Power.* New York: Basic, 2003.

Furneaux, Robin. *William Wilberforce.* London: Hamish Hamilton, 1974.

Galton, Francis. "Hereditary Improvement." *Fraser's Magazine* 7 (January–June 1873) 116–30.

Granville, Mary. *Autobiography and Correspondence of Mrs. Delaney,* 2 vols. Edited by Sarah Chauncey Woolsey. Boston: Roberts Brothers, 1880.

Guinness, Os. *The Call: Finding and Fulfilling the Central Purpose of Your Life.* Nashville: W, 2003.

Hague, William. *William Wilberforce: The Life of the Great Anti-Slave Trade Campaigner.* Orlando: Harcourt, 2007.

Hancock, Christopher D. "The 'Shrimp' Who Stopped Slavery." *Christian History* 16 (1997) 12–19.

Harding Alan. *The Countess of Huntingdon's Connexion: A Sect in Action in Eighteenth-Century England.* Oxford: Oxford University Press, 2003.

Harford, John S. *Recollections of William Wilberforce.* London: Longman, 1864.

Hind, Robert J. "William Wilberforce and the Perceptions of the British People." *Historical Research* 60 (1987) 321–25.

Hindmarsh, D. Bruce. *The Evangelical Conversion Narrative: Spiritual Autobiography in Early Modern England.* New York: Oxford University Press, 2005.

Hume, David. *Essays, Moral, Political, and Literary,* 2 vols. Edited by T. H. Green and T. H. Grose. London: Longmans, Green, 1898.

Inge, W. R. "Some Moral Aspects of Eugenics." *Eugenics Review* 1 (April 1909) 26–36.

Jones, Mary Gwladys. *Hannah More.* Cambridge: Cambridge University Press, 1952.

Kemp, N. D. A. *Merciful Release: The History of the British Euthanasia Movement* Manchester: Manchester University Press, 2002.

Kempis, Thomas á. *The Imitation of Christ.* Translated by Robert Jeffrey. London: Penguin, 2013.

Ker, Ian. *G. K. Chesterton: A Biography.* New York: Oxford University Press, 2011.

King, Martin Luther, Jr. *A Testament of Hope: The Essential Writings of Martin Luther King, Jr.* Edited by James Melvin Washington. San Francisco: Harper and Row, 1986.

Knutsford, Margaret. *Life and Letters of Zachary Macaulay.* London: Edward Arnold, 1900.

Kriegel, Abraham D. "A Convergence of Ethics: Saints and Whigs in British Antislavery." *Journal of British Studies* 26 (October 1987) 423–50.

Lambert, David. *Oswald Chambers.* Minneapolis: Bethany House, 1997.

Laski, H. J. "The Scope of Eugenics." *Westminster Review* 174 (1910) 25–34.

Laugesen, Amanda. *"Boredom is the Enemy": The Intellectual and Imaginative Lives of Australian Soldiers in the Great War and Beyond.* Farnham, UK: Ashgate, 2012.

Law, William. *A Serious Call To A Devout and Holy Life, Adapted to the State and Condition of All Orders of Christians.* Newcastle, UK: J. Barker, 1845.

Lewis, C. S. *Mere Christianity.* London: Macmillan, 1952.

———. *Surprised By Joy: The Shape of My Early Life.* New York: Harcourt, Brace and World, 1955.

McCasland, David. *Oswald Chambers: Abandoned to God.* Grand Rapids: Discovery House, 1993.

McKim, W. Duncan. *Heredity and Human Progress.* New York: Knickerbocker, 1901.

More, Hannah. *An Estimate of the Religion of the Fashionable World.* London: T. Cadell, 1791.

———. *Coelebs in Search of a Wife.* New York: Derby & Jackson, 1857.

———. *Poetical Works.* London: Scott, Webster, & Geary, 1838.

———. *The Works of Hannah More,* 7 vols. New York: Harper, 1843.

Newman, John Henry. "Selina, Countess of Huntingdon." In *Essays Critical and Historical,* 3rd ed., 386–424. London: Pickering, 1873.

Newton, John. *The Works of the Rev. John Newton,* 3rd ed., 6 vols. London: Hamilton, Adams, 1824.

Nuttall, Geoffrey F. "Howel Harris and the 'Grand Table': A Note on Religion and Politics 1744–50." *Journal of Ecclesiastical History* 39 (1988) 531–44.

Oddie, William. *Chesterton and the Romance of Orthodoxy: The Making of GKC 1874–1908.* Oxford: Oxford University Press, 2008.

Paine, Thomas. *The Works of Thomas Paine.* Philadelphia: James Carey, 1797.

Pearce, Joseph. *Wisdom and Innocence: A Life of G. K. Chesterton.* San Francisco: Ignatius, 1996.

Pollock, John. *Wilberforce.* New York: St. Martin's, 1977.

Potkay, Adam. "Olaudah Equiano and the Art of Spiritual Autobiography." *Eighteenth-Century Studies* 27 (Summer 1994) 677–92.

Randall, Ian M. "'Arresting People for Christ': Baptists and the Oxford Group in the 1930s." *Baptist Quarterly* 38 (January 1999) 3–18.

Reynolds, Barbara. *Dorothy L. Sayers: Her Life and Soul.* New York: St. Martin's, 1993.

Roberts, William. *Memoirs of the Life and Correspondence of Mrs. Hannah More,* 2 vols. New York: Harper Bros., 1836.

Robinson, William J. *Eugenics, Marriage and Birth Control.* New York: The Critic and Guide Company, 1917.

Sanger, Margaret. "The Eugenic Value of Birth Control Propaganda." *Birth Control Review* 5 (October 1921) 5.

Sayers, Dorothy. "The Church's Responsibility." In *Malvern, 1941: The Life of the Church and the Order of Society,* 57–78. London: Longmans, Green, 1941.

———. *Creed or Chaos?* Manchester, NH: Sophia Institute, 1996.

———. *Four Sacred Plays.* London: Gollancz, 1948.

———. *Gaudy Night.* London: Gollancz, 1935.

———. *The Letters of Dorothy L. Sayers,* 4 vols. Edited by Barbara Reynolds. New York: St. Martin's, 1996–2002.

———. *The Man Born to Be King.* New York: Harper, 1949.

———. *Mind of the Maker.* San Francisco: HarperSanFrancisco, 1979.

———. *Two Plays About God and Man.* Noroton, CT: Vineyard, 1977.

————. *Unnatural Death*. New York: Harper, 1955.

————. *Unpopular Opinions*. New York: Harcourt, Brace, 1947.

————, et al. "Vocation in Work." In *A Christian Basis for the Post-War World*, 89–105. New York: Morehouse-Gorham, 1942.

Schaeffer, Francis. *The God Who Is There*. Chicago: InterVarsity, 1968.

Schlenther, Boyd Stanley. *Queen of the Methodists: The Countess of Huntingdon and the Eighteenth-century Crisis of Faith and Society*. Durham, UK: Durham Academic Press, 1997.

Service with fighting men: an account of the work of the American Young Men's Christian Associations in the World War, 2 vols. Edited by William H. Taft, et al. New York: 1924.

Seymour, Aaron Crossan Hobart. *The Life and Times of Selina, Countess of Huntingdon: By a Member of the Houses of Shirley and Hastings*. London: W. E. Painter, 1844.

Shaw, George Bernard. *Major Barbara*. New York: Brentano's, 1907.

————. *The Revolutionist's Handbook, Man and Superman. A Comedy and a Philosophy* New York: Brentano's, 1903.

Shenstone, William. *Poetical Works*. London: J. Nisbet, 1854.

Simmons, Laura K. *Creed without Chaos: Exploring Theology in the Writings of Dorothy L. Sayers*. Grand Rapids: Baker Academic, 2005.

Snape, Michael. *The Back Parts of War: The YMCA Memoirs and Letters of Barclay Baron, 1915 to 1919*. Woodbridge, Rochester: Boydell, 2009.

Society for Bettering the Condition and Increasing the Comforts of the Poor. *Reports*, 40 vols. London: 1797–1817.

Spring, David. "The Clapham Sect: Some Social and Political Aspects." *Victorian Studies* 5 (September 1961) 35–48.

Stark, Gilbert Little. *Letters of Gilbert Little Stark*. Cambridge: Riverside, 1908.

Stone, Dan. *Breeding Superman: Nietzsche, Race and Eugenics in Edwardian and Interwar Britain*. Liverpool: Liverpool University Press, 2002.

Stopes, Marie. *Radiant Motherhood: A Book for Those Who Are Creating the Future*. London: Putnam's, 1920.

————, et al. *The Control of Parenthood*. New York: Putnam's, 1920.

Stott, Anne. *Hannah More: The First Victorian*. Oxford: Oxford University Press, 2003.

Thornton, Guy. *With the ANZACS in Cairo: The Tale of a Great Fight*. London: H. R. Allenson, 1916.

Tomkins, Stephen. *William Wilberforce: A Biography*. Grand Rapids: Eerdmans, 2007.

Tyerman, Luke. *The Life and Times of the Rev. John Wesley*, 3rd ed., 3 vols. London: Hodder and Stoughton, 1876.

Tyson, John R. "Lady Huntington's Reformation." *Church History* 64 (December 1995) 560–93.

Tyson, John R., and Boyd Stanley Schlenther, eds. *In the Midst of Early Methodism: Lady Huntingdon and Her Correspondence*. Lanham, MD: Scarecrow, 2006.

United Nations. "Universal Declaration of Human Rights." Online: http://www.un.org/en/documents/udhr/.

Walpole, Horace. *Private Correspondence of Horace Walpole*, 4 vols. London: Rodwell and Martin, 1820.

Walsh, John, Colin Haydon, and Stephen Taylor, eds. *The Church of England c. 1689–c. 1833: From Toleration to Tractarianism*. Cambridge: Cambridge University Press, 1993.

Walvin, James. *An African's Life: The Life and Times of Olaudah Equiano, 1745–1797.* London: Cassell, 1998.

Ward, Maisie. *Gilbert Keith Chesterton.* London: Sheed and Ward, 1944.

Welch, Edwin. "Lady Huntington and Spa Fields Chapel." *Guildhall Miscellany* 4 (1972) 175–83.

———. *Spiritual Pilgrim: A Reassessment of the Life of the Countess of Huntingdon.* Cardiff: University of Wales Press, 1995.

———, ed. *Two Calvinistic Methodist Chapels 1743–1811: The London Tabernacle and Spa Fields Chapel.* Leicester: London Record Society, 1975.

Wesley, John, *The Journal of John Wesley,* 2 vols. Edited by W. L. Watkinson. London: Kelly, 1903.

———. *The Letters of the Rev. John Wesley,* 8 vols. Edited by John Telford. London: Epworth, 1931.

———. *The Works of the Rev. John Wesley,* 7 vols. Edited by John Emory. New York: Carlton & Porter, 1856.

Wesley, John, and Charles Wesley. *The Poetical Works of John and Charles Wesley,* 13 vols. Edited by George Osborn. London: Wesleyan-Methodist Conference Office, 1868–1872.

White, Arnold. *Efficiency and Empire.* London: Methuen, 1901.

Whitehair, Charles W. *Out There.* New York: Appleton, 1918.

Wilberforce, Robert Isaac, and Samuel Wilberforce. *Life of William Wilberforce,* 5 vols. London: John Murray, 1838.

Wilberforce, William. *Correspondence of William Wilberforce,* 2 vols. Edited by Robert Isaac Wilberforce and Samuel Wilberforce. London: Murray, 1840.

———. *A Letter on the Abolition of the Slave Trade, Addressed to the Freeholders of Yorkshire.* London: Cadell, 1807.

———. *A Practical View of the Prevailing Religious System of Professed Christians in the Higher and Middle Classes of this Country Contrasted with Real Christianity.* London: Cadell, 1797.

———. *Private Papers.* Edited by A. M. Wilberforce. London: Unwin, 1897.

Wilkinson, Alan. "The Politics of the Anglican Modernists." *Chesterton Review* 15 (1989) 144–54.

Woodfin, Edward. *Camp and Combat on the Sinai and Palestine Front: The Experience of the British Empire Soldier, 1916–18.* Houndsmills, UK: Palgrave Macmillan, 2012.